How to cope with mid-life change

Janet Haines
Mandy Matthewson

Acknowledgements:
Steven Haines
Robyn Cartledge
Coverart designed by Freepik
(www.freepik.com)

This workbook offers suggestions on how to cope with midlife change. We do not guarantee that these suggested strategies will resolve all psychological symptoms. You may wish to seek alternative assistance from a mental health professional.

How to cope with mid-life change
Janet Haines & Mandy Matthewson
Copyright © 2025
ISBN: 978-1-923573-13-0

About the authors

Dr Janet Haines has a PhD in Clinical Psychology and has worked as an academic and researcher for 17 years, and in private practice for 30 years helping people facing life problems.

Dr Mandy Matthewson is a Clinical Psychologist, educator and researcher with more than two decades of experience supporting people through life's toughest challenges.

For those who woke up in midlife aching for a different story.
This is for the quiet, brave work of making changes to find new meaning and joy.

Table of contents

Table of contents 5
Introduction 8
What came before 9
    Successful life 9
    Worked hard 9
    Raised family 10
    Achieved status and financial success 11
    A carefree life 11
Then what happens? 13
    Feelings of discontent 13
    Anxiety 14
    Low mood 15
    Lack of satisfaction 15
    Poor quality of life 16
How do you react? 17
    The search for understanding 17
    Invalidation of your feelings 17
    Self-criticism 18
Triggers 19
    Work less interesting 19
    Children grown 20
    Sense of life passing 20
    A shocking event 21
What is going on? 23
    Shift in priorities 23
    Things that you once valued are no longer valuable 24
    Things got left by the wayside to focus on higher-value activities 24
A sense of self and identity 26
    What is a sense of self? 26
    Do I need a good sense of self? 26
    How does a good sense of self develop? 27
    How can I know my sense of self? 29
How should I react to what is happening to me? 33

- Understand the shift in priorities 33
- Normalise this experience 33
- Reprioritising things is acceptable 33

A way forward 34

Managing your anxiety 36
- What is my nervous system doing? 36
- Range of arousal 38

How to combat anxiety 41
- More exercises to help 47
- Managing anxiety-related thoughts 49

Regulating your emotions 54
- Primary and secondary emotions 54
- Recognising and dealing with your emotions 56
- Does the size of your emotion fit your problem? 60
- The link between emotions and behaviour 67

Setting reasonable expectations 71
- Setting expectations 71
- Language you use when talking to yourself 72
- Reframe your expectations in terms of preferences, not demands 74

Changing your thinking to manage your mood 77
- How are our thoughts affected? 77
- Core beliefs 78
- Cognitive errors 78
- Why do we think in unhelpful ways? 96
- Underlying assumptions of logical errors 98
- Understanding automatic thoughts 100
- Catching automatic thoughts 101
- Understanding and noticing logical errors 103
- Reframing your thoughts (cognitive restructuring) 105
- Making the restructured thinking habitual 109
- Targeting the assumptions 110

Restoring your sense of self 114
- How to build a strong sense of self 114

Improving your quality of life 120
- Values clarification exercise for choosing preferred activities 120

Planning a future 123
- Stages of change 123

Adopt a problem-solving approach	123
Building a flexible plan	127
Some final thoughts	129
Additional readings	130

Introduction

The purpose of this workbook is to help people who find themselves midway through their lives and are confused about the direction their lives should take. This can be difficult and confusing for those experiencing this uncertainty about the meaning and purpose of their lives.

This confusion can often occur despite there being no obvious reason for the stress you are feeling. For example, a successful professional who has worked hard and performed highly can find they are no longer satisfied with life. A mother who successfully and happily raised their children can find their life is now empty and unfulfilling.

Things can seem so wrong despite everything seemingly being fine, or at least when observed from the outside looking in. Typically, if you are feeling this way, you will look for explanations. For some, the reason will be obvious, but for others, they cannot find a reason for their unsettled feelings despite looking in all the usual places, that is, work, relationships, etc.

What came before

It is worthwhile to consider your life leading up to this point when dissatisfaction hits you. In general, you might find that you were happy enough with your life prior to your current dissatisfaction. It does not really matter whether your life followed a traditional pattern or an unconventional one; it is likely that things were going well enough up until this point.

Successful life

With the understanding that everyone has ups and downs in life, it is often the case that mid-life dissatisfaction occurs despite living a successful life until that point. The nature of that success is determined by the goals set by individuals and their personal wants and needs. People can pursue a particular career and succeed in reaching their career goals. Alternatively, others may have been happy focusing on other achievements in life, such as sporting, relationship, parenting or seeking experiences through travel, for example.

The point is that people who reach that point when they are confused and unsettled by their existing life may have had a satisfactory life before that occurred. A successful life does not prevent the development of dissatisfaction at some other time.

> *Lydia is a successful lawyer. She had worked hard throughout her life to achieve the goal of being a partner in her law firm. She had done well at uni and had worked in casual jobs to pay her way throughout her law studies. After starting work in law, she was driven to succeed. Not only had she done well in her chosen career, Lydia had achieved all the other normal life ambitions she had chosen for herself. She married and had two children. With the help of her husband, who was less ambitious than she had been, she had been able to work long hours and at least part of most weekends. She viewed herself as successful and had been proud of her career achievements. However, things changed. She struggled to find the motivation to go to work and to focus on the cases that previously would have excited her. At first, Lydia thought there was something physically wrong with her that would explain why she was feeling so disinterested and lethargic. Despite undertaking a range of medical tests, her doctor could find nothing wrong with her. Slowly, Lydia came to realise that she didn't like her job anymore. The things she had wanted most in her life just weren't of interest to her anymore.*

Worked hard

The confusing nature of the mid-life questioning of the purpose of your life can derive from the extent to which you have worked hard to achieve what you have in life. This may be through seeking relevant qualifications for your career, devoting yourself to a caring or nurturing role, or working to achieve specific goals. When you devote that amount of effort to something that is so important to you at the time, it can be confronting to question whether what you have achieved is what you now want.

> *Daniel had been busy for as long as he could remember. He has a demanding job working as a personal assistant to a very successful and demanding boss who runs her own company. His working life is high-powered and fast-paced. There are lots of personal advantages to his job. He gets to travel with his boss. He attends many of the social engagements to which his boss is invited. To maintain his usefulness to his boss and, therefore, his job, Daniel has been working very long hours. He rarely has a day off. His job was exciting, and he had always wanted to ensure that he could keep this amazing job for as long as he wanted. Although he is paid very well for what he does, Daniel has started to question whether it is worth it. He has been thinking about what he has missed out on in life by being available seven days a week to ensure his boss' needs are met. He is sick of the travel, and the parties and social events no longer seem as exciting as they had previously. On the one hand, Daniel knew he had a job many people would strongly desire. On the other hand, Daniel has been questioning whether he still wants this job. These thoughts frighten Daniel. He keeps wondering what he would do if he wasn't at his boss' beck and call.*

Raised family

Your adult life may have been devoted to raising your children by nurturing them and preparing them for their adult lives. In all likelihood, this would have been a rewarding undertaking for many. This type of dedication to parenting can be consuming. Other choices you make and demands on your time may have been arranged around your parenting activities.

This type of dedication can cause you to question your role in life when the need to be so present in your children's lives is reduced. This is inevitable in most cases. You spend years preparing your children for adulthood. However, their increased independence and self-sufficiency can leave you searching for a new role in life.

> *When Ben and Katie started a family, they were clear about what sort of parents they wanted to be. They wanted to give their children the best start in life, so they devoted their lives to raising them. Ben worked hard but still managed to dedicate time to spend with the children when he returned home from work. He attended all of the children's extracurricular activities on the weekends. Katie gave up her job when the children were small, returning to part-time work when they commenced school. She always picked them up from school and would take them to weekday activities after school on the days when these activities were scheduled. School holidays were filled with child-friendly activities.*

> *As the children got older and needed less of their parents' time, Ben transitioned easily and found activities that met his own needs. He started playing golf with a friend, arranged to catch up with mates, and joined a community-based group that worked on projects to improve their neighbourhood. In contrast, Katie struggled. She had a job that didn't really fulfil her desire to do something useful, she struggled to think of things she wanted to do, and she had too many hours that seemed to be without direction. Although she was happy enough when she spent time with Ben, at other times, she realised she was deeply unhappy about her life now that the children were living independently.*

Achieved status and financial success

You are not protected from confusion and dissatisfaction with life by high status or financial success. Typically, these achievements require focused attention and devotion of your time over an extended period of time. This can mean that you may have missed out on other things in life. You may have been willing to sacrifice these other things while climbing the ladder. However, you may question whether that sacrifice was worth it when you see others with things that you would like to have but have not pursued because of your attention to other goals.

> *For as long as she could remember, Eloise had craved financial success. As a teenager, she managed to get a number of jobs, always moving on to a better-paid position as her skill set grew. She knew she wanted a highly paid job, so she selected university studies that were likely to give her the opportunities to maximise her chances of obtaining well-paid positions. By the time she started work in her chosen career, Eloise had sufficient money saved to use as a deposit to purchase a house. She then rented this property and bought another. Her property portfolio grew over time to an impressive degree. Eloise then took a calculated risk and started a business of her own, initially working on it on a part-time basis and then, as it grew, working full-time. By the time she turned forty, Eloise was a wealthy woman by anyone's standards. However, Eloise suddenly realised she had no real friends. She knew lots of people, but there was no one in her life who she considered to be close to her. Relationships had come and gone. But she never really had the time for these partners or to develop friendships. Relationships and friendships seemed like a distraction from her goal of being financially well off. When she turned forty and took time to reflect on her life, Eloise realised she was lonely and had been for a long time.*

A carefree life

Prior to this point in your life, you may have had a carefree existence. Your preference may have been to pursue a life without some of the responsibilities that other people take on.

You may have chosen to travel, live from day to day, or not 'settle down'. Rather than following a more traditional pathway, you may have chosen a more unconventional one. However, as time goes by, you may start to question your choices and think about what you do not have rather than the value of the things you have experienced until this point in your life.

> *Matthew had spent his life as a young adult doing what he wanted. He would pick up some work here and there, earning enough to get him to his next travel destination. He never had much money, but he had travelled to places outside of normal tourist destinations. He had many stories to tell of his travels. Matthew also liked to party. He liked to live a life as a carefree and single person. He had no fixed abode and few possessions, but he had always been happy doing what he had chosen. He relied on the goodwill of others and moved from place to place, sleeping wherever he happened to land. If you had asked Matthew, he would have said that he was happy and that his life was fulfilling... until it wasn't. Matthew started to notice that everyone living the same sort of life was younger than him. All of the travel and partying started to seem less exciting. He started to yearn for something more. So, Matthew came home to visit his family and catch up with friends from his past. He found that most of his friends had very different lives than his own. They were married with children and had good jobs. They were living settled lives and seemed happy. Although they were interested in hearing about Matthew's travels, Matthew realised they were not in any way envious. In fact, Matthew found that he was the one who was envious of the lives his friends were living. This was unsettling for Matthew, who believed he would never want what they had in life.*

People's lives are a culmination of a range of the individual events they experience. In this way, although there can be similarities between people's lives, each person has their own unique experience. The point that needs to be made here is not that one person's life is not like another person's life. It is that people can live a life that is satisfactory for them until their feelings, opinions, and perspectives change. It is this change that is unsettling for people and can be unexpected.

Then what happens?

It is the case that people can experience their life, however that occurs, in a manner that is satisfactory until they reach a point where they are no longer satisfied or comfortable with the life they have chosen, or aspects of the life they have chosen. This change can trigger a range of reactions in people.

Feelings of discontent

If you are confused and questioning whether your life is satisfactory and of good quality, these feelings can be triggered by a more general feeling of discontent. This feeling of discontent can be especially difficult to understand if there are no obvious indicators of why you should feel this way. After all, to this point, you have probably been living the life you chose.

In response to these feelings, you can start to search for meaning. That is, you start to ask yourself why you feel this way. In an effort to understand, you can blame the wrong things. For example, if you are feeling unsettled, you might look to your relationship and blame your discontent on a relationship which is the one that sustained you through your earlier life. You may identify your children becoming more independent as the cause of your problem despite you spending their whole lives preparing them for this very thing.

The cause of the discontent is actually quite simple. It occurs because your life is not the way you would like it to be at this point in time. The confusing aspect of it may be that the life you are now questioning may have been entirely satisfactory earlier on.

However, it is not particularly unusual that what you want in life has changed. The fact of the matter is that we change, grow and develop throughout our lives. We tend to understand this in children. For example, a five-year-old's needs are not the same as a fifteen-year-old's needs. Their way of looking at and understanding the world is different. This is accepted, and no one questions it. We spend less time considering that what we want at age 25 years might not be what we want at 45 years, 65 years, or 85 years of age.

Daniel was feeling very unsettled. He couldn't find any pleasure in any aspect of his life. He felt tired and fed up with all the things that used to matter to him. He knew he wasn't depressed. There was something else going on. It wasn't that he hated his job... but he didn't get excited about it like he used to feel. He knew he loved his children, but he struggled to be interested in their day-to-day lives, and this made him feel guilty. He supposed he loved his wife, but he didn't feel the attraction to her that he had previously felt. She seemed settled on her path in life and didn't seem to need him as much anymore. Matthew tried to make sense of why he was feeling this way. He lay awake at night,.

> *churning over in his mind all of the aspects of his life and how things seemed to have ended up feeling so wrong. He knew something had to change. He needed to work, and he had a responsibility to his children. Daniel began to wonder if it would make his life better if he left his marriage. In an attempt to address his confusing dissatisfaction, Daniel was almost talking himself into marital separation as an answer to his problem. Rather than seeing that his ambivalence about his relationship was a symptom of the problem, he was thinking his relationship was the cause of his problem*

Anxiety

These feelings of discontent and the confusion they create can make you feel anxious. The reason for this is simple. We cope less well when things are uncertain. We feel off-balance and unsettled, and without a clear indication of why this is occurring, we experience anxiety.

We will be discussing anxiety more later. At this point, it is worth knowing that when you feel anxiety without an obvious cause, your brain will go looking for an explanation. You start to question things that would otherwise be considered to be fine.

Also, because you are experiencing anxiety, and you should really only feel anxious when there is a cause, you develop a sense that something terrible is looming. The part of your nervous system that causes the anxiety should only be activated if there is a threat to you. In the absence of that threat, you can still feel that there is an imminent threat, even if there is no threat.

For some women who are facing mid-life changes, the hormonal changes that can be the result of pre-menopausal and peri-menopausal states can influence how unsettled you feel and exacerbate feelings of anxiety. It can be difficult to accurately attribute the cause of your anxiety when there are multiple contributing factors.

> *Evelyn couldn't make sense of what was happening. She had always been a confident person. She had always been able to deal with her problems and the challenges life threw in her path. In general, she considered herself to be optimistic, self-sufficient and determined. And that is why she was confused. Seemingly out of the blue, Evelyn had begun to feel anxious. It started out as a niggly feeling of unease but had developed into a raging anxiety that she could not quell. On paper, everything in her life was fine. She had a supportive husband, her children were happy and well, she had friends, she had a job she had always liked, and she had no particular health problems. But she could not shake this anxiety. She believed the anxiety she was experiencing was causing her to feel unhappy about her life in general. Rather than seeing that the anxiety she was feeling was because*

> *there was something she needed to address, Evelyn believed that if she could just make her anxiety go away, everything would return to normal. She started a war with her anxiety, battling her symptoms with a determination to win. She couldn't understand why this wasn't working.*

Low mood

Your mood can be affected by ongoing feelings of unrest and discontent. The things that used to give you pleasure seem not to offer you that type of experience anymore.

With the important things in your life no longer being available or not being of as high a value to you as they used to be, much of the reward in your life is reduced. This reduction in reward often leads to a low mood. There is too little of what matters to you happening in your life.

This lack of reward that leads to a low mood can create problems of motivation. It is hard to feel enthusiastic about things in your life if you do not feel engaged with them and they do not offer you the same stimulation and interest as used to be the case.

> *Usually an energetic and enthusiastic person, Bronwyn was finding it difficult to force herself to get out of bed. She was sleeping more than usual, and she was also spending time just laying in bed staring at nothing in particular. When she wasn't in bed, she was dragging herself through the day. She was finding it hard to feel any excitement about the things that had previously motivated her. Bronwyn thought that it wasn't that she felt sad. It was more the case that she felt numb. Despite understanding that this is how she felt, she couldn't put a finger on a reason why she felt this way. She never had before, and there was nothing in her life that had changed. For Bronwyn, everything that used to matter to her no longer did so. She just didn't understand how her life had lost its purpose.*

Lack of satisfaction

Although we have been mentioning the lack of satisfaction throughout our discussion so far, it is worth mentioning it further here. It can be the case that this general lack of satisfaction with life can cause you to become focused on the uncertainty you currently are experiencing. It can also be the case that this life dissatisfaction can cause you to focus more on how you are feeling, including your symptoms of anxiety and low mood.

> *Kevin was feeling bad. He was finding it difficult to experience any pleasure in the things he was doing in life. Typically, he was a person who had an active life full of interesting and challenging aspects. He always prided himself on being fully engaged with his life. But, for months, Kevin had been feeling almost annoyed with his life. In general, he felt irritated and even small things would aggravate this feeling. It seemed that nothing pleased him anymore. And that was all he could think about. Kevin was feeling bad, and focusing on how he was feeling was making him feel worse.*

Poor quality of life

When you are going through a period in mid-life when the things you value no longer seem important or are no longer available to you, the quality of your life tends to change. As stated, things seem less rewarding, your life feels less satisfying, you feel anxious and confused, and your mood is low. In effect, you no longer feel content. Instead, you feel that something is missing or wrong. Without enough in your life that matters to you, the quality of your life can be poor.

> *Aiden used to feel quite content about his life. He thought he had a happy balance between his work and home life. However, if he was honest, recently, he realised he had spent too much of this time promoting his career and too little time on other aspects of his life. He rarely saw his friends, had little time for his family, and paid too little attention to his loyal and patient wife. It was confronting for Aiden to realise his life wasn't nearly as balanced as he had thought. And it wasn't nearly as rewarding as he wanted it to be. Aiden didn't know what to do to make things better. He felt stuck in the life he had made for himself. The responsibilities he had at work made him feel trapped and unable to just walk away.*

What we see is that the changes people face that divert them from one path in their lives to another can be unsettling. You think you have been doing what you chose to do, and you are correct. However, the fact that this is no longer enough or no longer the right thing for you can throw you off balance.

How do you react?

The fact that your life is no longer as satisfying for you as it has been in the past (or the fact that you have been able to ignore the dissatisfaction) causes you to rethink your situation. In recognising that you feel unsettled and off-balance, there are a number of things you might do in reaction to this knowledge.

The search for understanding

This can be a very confusing time for people. You believe that you understand what you are doing, what your life means and where you are going. Then, you find yourself questioning what is happening and where you are heading. It can seem that you have gone from having a life where things were all right to existing with uncertainty and unpredictability.

This confusion can trigger a search for understanding. You start to examine aspects of your life that might give you a clue about why you are feeling so unsettled. For some, it will be obvious, and the cause will be easily identifiable. For other people, this search can take them down blind alleys. In trying to understand, you start to examine all aspects of your life, even those areas that are not directly responsible for your current state. You can begin to question whether your perception of various aspects of your life is accurate.

> *Joshua needed to understand what was happening to him. He felt so unlike himself that he was worried. At first, he thought there must be something physically wrong with him. However, a trip to the doctor didn't identify any signs of ill health. He then wondered if something was wrong with his relationship with his wife. After giving this consideration, he felt that he was as committed to his marriage as he had always been. He wondered whether his job was the problem. He knew he didn't feel as enthusiastic about his career as he had been at its outset, but this lack of interest didn't feel important enough to have triggered this feeling he had that something wasn't right. In truth, he just felt like he was unlike himself, and he couldn't figure out the cause. This lack of understanding made him feel even more unsettled. He knew he couldn't go on feeling like this, but he needed to be able to put his finger on what was wrong so he could fix it.*

Invalidation of your feelings

As a result of your confusion about what is happening in your life and the reasons for that confusion, you can start to question the validity of your emotional state. You can invalidate your feelings in a couple of ways. For example, you may choose to ignore your feelings and what they are trying to tell you. You can pretend to be happy when you are not feeling that way. You can pretend that you are content and feeling in control when you feel anything but these emotions.

Also, you may reject your feelings as invalid. You can be aware that you are feeling bad but then tell yourself that you have no right to feel that way. You look at your life, what you have achieved, and how things are going in general and conclude that you have no right to feel discontented. In this way, you create a battle between what your head is telling you (i.e., everything is going well in your life) and what your emotional state is telling you (i.e., I am upset and discontented).

> *Gemma knew she had a good life. She had a partner who loved her, and her children were happy and healthy. She had good and loyal friends. She was fit and healthy. She had a good job, and she was held in high regard in her workplace. She was financially secure and had enough money for travel and luxuries that she knew other people couldn't afford. But Gemma was unhappy, and although she couldn't put her finger on why, when she reflected on the matter, she knew she was not content. So, she stopped reflecting. She thought she had no right to complain. She knew terrible things were happening in the world, and she was aware that other people were suffering because of the real things they were experiencing. Gemma thought she did not have the right to complain about her life, which must seem so perfect compared with the lives of others. She thought it was better to ignore these feelings of discontent and just be grateful for what she had. And, for much of the time, she could ignore her discontent... but not always.*

Self-criticism

On paper, you may see that you have a life that other people desire, yet you feel dissatisfied with life. As a result, you can feel that you are not justified in feeling the way you do. The consequence of this is that you start to be self-critical. You can tell yourself that you *should not* feel the way you do even though you recognise that you do feel that way. You criticise yourself for feeling unsettled. You can feel ungrateful and disconnected.

> *Austin reached the conclusion he wasn't a very good person. This was because he was dissatisfied with a life that most people would envy. So, he got into a habit of berating himself every time something good happened to him. He told himself that he didn't deserve anything good coming his way, even though he had worked hard for his achievements. He criticised himself for gaining things he felt he did not deserve because he didn't appreciate them. He also criticised himself for feeling so disinterested in and unappreciative of the life he had built for himself and his family. Of course, none of this self-criticism caused him to feel more content.*

So, you can react in a variety of ways to the fact that the pathway you have chosen in life (or was thrust upon you) is no longer the one you want. None of these reactions feel good, and none help you fix the problem. In any case, it is hard to fix a problem that you do not fully understand, and you cannot pinpoint the cause.

Triggers

There are a multitude of reasons for a difficult period in your middle life. Some are simple and straightforward. Others are more complicated and can involve factors that were established a long time before the problems you are currently facing commenced. But what happened to cause the change right now?

Work less interesting

You may have reached where you want to be in life after working hard over many years. You may even have focused on work to the exclusion of other domains in your life, such as family or leisure. However, you can then find that work is no longer interesting. It does not provide you with the sense of satisfaction that you previously felt.

This can be a very disturbing experience, to feel that the thing you have worked so hard for is no longer giving you what you want in life. Going to work is harder than it has been in the past. You can feel less enthusiasm for your work tasks. You can start to question why you are doing what you are doing. You can feel despondent thinking about a future where you are facing more years of the same job that is no longer meaningful for you.

> *Rebecca was a medical specialist. She had worked hard during her training to obtain the qualifications she had achieved. She then went on to establish a private practice and also worked within the public health system. She was highly regarded and considered an expert in her field. She had previously been very enthusiastic about her job. However, Rebecca began to feel nothing but disinterest. Although she continued to do a good job and worked for her patients to the best of her ability, she found herself caring less about them as individuals. She felt pressured by the other demands made on her in her professional life, such as giving talks or training sessions for new doctors in her field. She wanted to be left alone. Rebecca dreamed of making chutneys and relishes and selling them at the local weekend market. She wanted to have the time to grow the produce she would need. She wanted a simple, uncomplicated life that would allow her to do as she chose when she chose to do it. Rebecca kept these thoughts to herself. She knew that others would never understand her desire to give up her hard-earned career and the financial benefits it provided for this simpler life. She believed that others would see her as irresponsible if she gave up this career, given her ability to help others in her current job. Whenever she thought about a different, preferred life, she felt like crying because it seemed impossible to achieve.*

Children grown

Child rearing and the role of a parent can be fulfilling and all-consuming for many people. Your children's needs are put before your own, and you do this willingly. It is a choice you make when you prioritise your role as a parent over other aspects of your life. Your activities are family-focused, and financial decisions take into account the children's needs, but your own needs seem less important relative to your commitment to your children.

However, what happens when your children need you less? You have spent your parenting years preparing your children for independence and self-sufficiency. It is an important goal of parenting. Nevertheless, you may be ill-prepared for the time when your children are ready and able to express that independence from you. Your largest and most consuming role in your life is diminished and continues to reduce to a point where you have too much time available that would normally be used caring for your children.

For some people, this normal experience of their children becoming more independent of them can lead them to feel lost. What motivates them each day is no longer available to them. This can be very disconcerting. It makes people feel adrift. With very limited experience in meeting their own needs and putting themselves first, people in this position can feel lost and uncertain about what to do to change their life circumstances.

> *Stacey had always been considered to be a good mother. She worked hard to make sure her children had everything they needed. She was an active participant in their lives, and she revelled in the joy they brought her. The majority of her time and attention had been on them throughout their childhood years. And now they were gone, living their own independent lives. They were pursuing their careers, exploring relationships and making decisions for themselves. They were the people she had raised them to be. Her family and friends expected Stacey to be happy now that she had more time for herself. They seemed to be waiting to see what she would do next now that the children were old enough to function independently of her. But Stacey had no idea what to do. She just felt like there was a huge hole in her life that used to be filled with the noise and love and interest her children's presence offered her. She didn't know what to do about the hole. She looked at other people's lives and couldn't see anything that interested her. Stacey was feeling a bit panicky. The thought of endless years to come without her previous role in life was more than she could bear. The only thing that cheered her was the idea that, sometime in the future, she would hopefully be a grandmother and she could help raise these children. She had no clue what she was going to do in the meantime.*

Sense of life passing

In the absence of any other, more evident reason for feeling unsettled about your life, it may be that your emotional state is being caused by a sense that life is moving on and your opportunities for making changes, seeking new horizons, and pursuing new ambitions have passed. You can develop a sense that there is nothing left in life to look forward to or work towards.

Alternatively, you may feel that life is passing and you have missed the chance to achieve significant life goals that you always thought you would achieve. You can develop a sense of running out of time.

> *Theo woke up one morning and realised that he was middle-aged. The thought hit him like a bolt of lightning. He calculated how many years he was likely to have left in his life and how much time he had out of those years to still be active and able to do all the things he wanted to do. He thought about how quickly time had passed and how quickly the coming years would likely pass. These thoughts just wouldn't go away, no matter how much he tried to push them from his mind. He made lists in his mind of all the things he had wanted to do throughout his life but had put off for one reason or another. He had always assumed there would be time, and there would come a day when he could choose to do things other than work and care for his family. He berated himself for postponing things in his life that he had considered were important but believed could be achieved in the future. Theo felt a strange combination of emotions that he had never felt before. It was a mix of resentment, fear and desperation. He thought that if he had any chance of doing the things he had always planned to do, he would have to turn his current life upside down. This made him feel frightened, too. From the outside, it looked like he was the same person doing the same things he did every day. Inside, he felt like he was screaming.*

A shocking event

The sense of needing to adjust one's life can be triggered by a single, shocking event. These types of events can give us what is termed a 'sense of a fore-shortened future'. Usually, we carry on in life like tomorrow will happen and, the day after that, and the day after that. However, something big can occur, and our belief that tomorrow will happen with a good degree of certainty is shaken. We can develop a sense of urgency to do more in the limited time available in case it is all taken away from us. We can also develop a sense that there is no point in doing anything because tomorrow may never come.

> *Greg learned that his friend from his school days was killed in a terrible workplace accident. Although they hadn't kept in close contact, Greg had run into his friend from time to time over the years. He had met his friend's wife and knew his friend had teenaged children. Greg attended his friend's funeral and listened to those talking about the tragedy of someone losing their life so prematurely. Since learning of his friend's death, Greg couldn't stop thinking about all the things his friend will never get to do. Greg also thought about all the things he would miss out on doing if something ever happened to him. Greg started to feel anxious. He considered all the things he thought he would do in the future and worried that he would never get around to doing them. He wondered why he was working so hard when he could be doing things he enjoyed more than his work. He thought he should reprioritise what was important to him. Greg's wife worried about this change in Greg and fretted about what was going to happen if Greg stopped working. While his wife was worried about their future financial security, Greg was worried he would not have a future. The difference in their concerns was causing some friction between them.*

These are examples of the types of things that can trigger adjustment problems that can occur in mid-life. They are not the only reasons. This is because people are complex creatures, and their lives are unique to them. These examples do give you an idea of how both unexpected things and usual and anticipated things can still trigger a shift in your view of your life.

What is going on?

You are justified in asking yourself why you do not just acknowledge the fact that you are examining your life and then get on with things. You ask yourself why this reflection on your life is causing you such difficulty. Let's consider some explanations for why this is a bigger thing than you had expected to happen in your life.

Shift in priorities

We prioritise things in life. It is clearly the case that there are times in our lives when some things are important, whereas they are less important at other times in life. So, the things that are important to us can change across our lifespans. This can be strongly apparent when we consider what we wanted in our teenage years compared with what we might want later in life.

Interestingly, we tend to understand that our needs and wants can change rapidly in our early years. We are tolerant of this and see it as normal development. However, we tend to understand it less well later in life. So, we have less understanding of developmental changes across our entire lifespan. We feel that once we are on our adult pathway, that is where we will stay. Of course, this is not the case. We are as capable of shifting priorities or wanting change at later points in our lives as we are in our early stages of life.

> *Brandon had always wanted to have his own business. He had always wanted to be his own boss. In the early days, he worked for other people, but only so that he could develop expertise and gain a good financial foundation to allow him to go out on his own. As soon as he could, that is what he did. He started his own business. In the beginning, he worked long hours to get the business up and running. It had been stressful at times, but it had also been exciting. All the hard work had paid off. His business grew and was successful. Brandon had what he had always wanted – a successful business. Brandon was surprised that, after years of working for himself, he was tired of the responsibility and the stressors that came with being the person in charge. Even though he had people working for him, Brandon found he was still working long hours. The pressure on him was unrelenting. He was never able to take a break or go on a holiday. At the end of each day, he couldn't just turn off his work life. What had always seemed so important to him was no longer desirable. It was surprising to him that he wanted other things in life. He now wanted less responsibility, more leisure time, and more fun. He wanted someone other than him to be in charge and to worry about all the day-to-day aspects of running a business. He realised the business was no longer important to him.*

Things that you once valued are no longer valuable

As a result of the shift in priorities that you might experience, things that you once viewed as being highly important can no longer seem so. Intellectually you may see that the activities are important but, emotionally, you cease to appreciate their value. With this change in perceived value, you find it difficult to devote time and attention to activities that are low priority to you.

It is worth understanding that what you value in life may be different from what other people value. It is all right to make the choices you make about the direction of your life based on the things that matter to you, even if they differ from what others want. It is also quite normal for the things that you value in life to change over the course of your lifespan.

> *Jenny loved to party. She loved to go to nightclubs, hang out with her friends, drink too much alcohol and dance. She spent her weekdays looking forward to the weekends. She spent too many days battling with having too little sleep the night before. She had brief relationships but never really settled down with one person. It was a lifestyle that Jenny loved, and she thought she would never want it to change. Her life was fun. However, over time, Jenny started to change. She found herself longing for stability and predictability. She became interested in setting up a comfortable home for herself. She enjoyed decorating her home and working in her garden. She wasn't really aware of these changes, and if she was, she didn't pay them much attention. That is, she didn't notice the changes until one day, she entered a raffle to raise money for a charity. The prize was a wheelbarrow full of snack food and bottles of alcohol. Jenny had the winning ticket, and her first thought was, "Good, I need a new wheelbarrow". Jenny started to laugh, realising how completely the importance of things in her life had shifted.*

Things got left by the wayside to focus on higher-value activities

When you prioritise certain activities or areas in your life, it is normal and understandable that these activities take up most of your time and attention. However, it does mean that other areas of your life that you may consider valuable are left unattended. There can then come a point in your life when you realise you have missed out on these things that you have ignored up to this point.

Alternatively, you have been focused on some things that were important to you, but they were pushed down your priority list as other interests or responsibilities needed your attention. At some point, you can feel like you have lost some things that were once very important to you. This realisation can be difficult.

> *Victoria was a ballroom dance sport champion. She had started dancing when she was a small child. She had won national and international championships. To achieve this level of success, Victoria had devoted all her spare time to dancing. As a child, she had dance practice after school most days, and she competed on the weekends. As an adult, she had various jobs that paid the bills but ones that did not distract her from her dancing. She practised with her dance partner and her dance coaches but had little time for friendships outside of the dance world and even less time for romantic relationships. By the time she was in her mid-thirties, Victoria had achieved at the highest levels and was generally considered to set a standard of excellence few others could aspire to reach. Victoria told people that she lived to dance. That had been true for many years, but even though she continued to say this, she knew it was no longer true. Something that had mattered to her so much no longer was of interest to her. She was tired, disinterested and simply couldn't be bothered putting in the effort that was needed to stay at the top. Victoria didn't know what she wanted to do instead, but she did know that she had started to envy the people who had more balanced and settled lives. She began to believe that she had wasted her time giving all of her attention to dance. This was confusing for Victoria. How could something that had mattered so much now matter so little?*

When you look at the things that contribute to your current unsettled feelings, they seem to make sense. They are quite reasonable and, in lots of ways, manageable. However, they seem to have the capacity to throw you off balance, cause you to lose that sense of certainty about who you are, and cause you to feel unsettled.

A sense of self and identity

The loss of certainty about who you are and where your life is heading can be very unsettling. We are referring here to a loss of your sense of self and loss of certainty about your identity.

What is a sense of self?

Your 'sense of self' refers to your understanding of the various characteristics that define who you are as a person. What contributes to your sense of self can include more permanent characteristics such as personality traits as well as less stable features. These might include your skills and abilities, such as what you are good at, what you like and dislike, what you believe in or your philosophical view of life and the world, your moral and ethical codes, and the things that inspire or motivate you. Put together, these are the features that make you an individual and define your identity.

People who have a strong sense of self can readily identify these features about themselves. They know who they are and what they stand for. Others, with a less well-defined sense of self, might struggle to know what it is that matters to them or what they view as important to them.

Do I need a good sense of self?

Most people do not spend a lot of time thinking about their sense of self. Nevertheless, your sense of self can still have an impact on you. A clearly defined sense of self gives your life purpose because you understand the reasons you choose to do things. It can also help in other areas of your life, such as relationships, and these influences contribute to better emotional well-being.

Knowing yourself well can make it easier for you to accept both your positive attributes and the things you are proud of, as well as things about yourself that are not satisfactory and may require some work. It is easier to address those unsatisfactory attributes when you have a stronger sense of self because that knowledge of who you are will direct you to make changes. If your sense of self is not as strong, it is hard to know what you want and, therefore, harder to know what direction to take to make changes.

Without a strong sense of self, you tend to drift through life. You are more likely to be influenced by what others want or what others decide you should be doing. This can result in a general feeling of discontent, never feeling certain about who you are, separate from other people's view of you.

How does a good sense of self develop?

The development of our sense of self can be influenced by a range of factors. Without these influences, it may be harder to have a strong sense of self. This is not to say that a sense of self cannot be achieved. However, it does mean that those people who have a less certain idea of who they are, may not have had the advantage of some of these influences.

Let's consider a few of these factors.

Encouragement to be yourself

From childhood, some people are encouraged to be individuals. This process of individuation is encouraged by parents and care-providers allowing children to explore their environment and make their needs known. The children are encouraged to learn and to make mistakes in a supported environment. These children are more likely to develop a good sense of self.

For other children, any attempt to express themselves from their own perspective is met with less encouragement. Self-expression may be punished or criticised, or it may be ignored. As a result of the negative response a child can receive for being themselves, they may choose the easier option of doing and being what others demand or expect of them. Without the type of encouragement we are talking about here, a child may not develop a strong sense of self.

> *Donald, an engineer, was sitting at his desk drawing up plans for his client for a sewage system for a development project. It struck him how unhappy he had been for as long as he could remember. He realised that he did not want to be an engineer and, as far as he could remember, had never wanted to be an engineer. However, this was the career his parents had chosen for him. They thought engineering was a good job, and any talk of other interests was dismissed. As a teen, Donald liked music, art, and woodwork, but his parents insisted that he would never have a stable job if he pursued training in these areas. By the time Donald was about to start university, he hadn't even bothered telling his parents that he wanted to obtain a Fine Arts degree in furniture design. He knew they would never support this. Donald just accepted that it was a foregone conclusion that he would train to become an engineer. Now that he was working in this area, Donald was very unhappy.*

Attachment

The nature of your relationship with your parents or caregivers may influence how your sense of self develops. We are referring here to the nature of your attachment and whether or not it is secure. Secure attachment during childhood helps a child grow into an adult who can develop close relationships, who can give and receive support and comfort when needed, and who can engage in flexible and cooperative behaviour.

If you did not have a secure attachment, it is likely that you were uncertain about whether or not love and nurturance would be provided to you. A child in this situation can come to learn that they need to act in a way that meets their parents' or caregivers' needs so that they receive approval. In this way, children will shape themselves into the people that others want them to be rather than being themselves. A strong sense of self may not develop, and this can then affect adult relationships because, as adults, these people will continue to be the people their partner wants them to be rather than being themselves.

> *In lots of ways, Ellen and her husband were very different. He was extroverted, active and outdoorsy. If she was being honest with herself, Ellen would say that she was more at peace with quiet introspection and intellectual pursuits. But she never told anyone this and didn't let her thoughts go down this pathway very often. Instead, she did what made her husband happy. She joined him in his social engagements. She learned to scuba dive, she went fishing, and she bushwalked and abseiled. She did all of these things to the exclusion of the things she would prefer to be doing. In fact, it is doubtful that her husband would even have been aware that she wasn't interested in these shared activities, and she would prefer not to engage in them. He didn't know because Ellen didn't tell him. She was too frightened to do so. She worried that if her husband knew she didn't share the same love of his preferred activities, he would leave her. Indeed, Ellen always felt that her relationship with her husband was uncertain. No matter how much he tried to reassure her that he loved her and wanted to be with her, and no matter how many times he asked her what she wanted to do, Ellen felt she could not risk losing him by speaking up and telling him she might like to try other activities.*

Fitting in with peers

Adolescents may try to model themselves to the peers they most admire. This is especially so for teens who struggle to fit in with their peer group. They will observe the behaviour of more confident peers or those who have interpersonal skills that make them seem confident. They will then try to copy these behaviours in an effort to make themselves more like these admired individuals.

This can present a problem. A teen in this situation may have to change repeatedly to fit into the group they have associated themselves with at any given point in time. As a result, they tend to lose sight of who they are as individuals, what they want, and how to make choices to suit their own needs.

This can continue into adulthood. For example, you may take on the role of a certain type of employee at work that is different from who you are at home with your family. You may then act in a completely different way when you are with your friends. You can get into a pattern where you are constantly searching for a persona that suits the situation you are in at the time. It is hard to develop a good sense of self when you are trying to be like everyone else.

> *If you asked Douglas' family what he was like, they would say that he was a quiet and thoughtful man who was always respectful of others. His parents would describe him as a fine man who had a value system that was consistent with the way they had raised him. His wife would describe him in a similar way. She would add that he was very protective of her and she always felt safe and secure in her relationship with him. She knew that she could rely on her husband. She would also tell you that he was a good father who focused on instilling in their children a good value system. His wife and family assumed that this was how Douglas always was in any circumstance or situation. However, that was not the case. Douglas worked in a male-dominated workplace with a group of 'blokes'. They would say that Doug was 'one of them'. He liked off-colour jokes; he was loud and a bit of a clown. If you asked Douglas to describe himself, he would have been hard-pressed to give you a good account of what he was like.*

How can I know my sense of self?

So, where do you start to try to understand your sense of self? With it being something you rarely think about, it is hard to know what you should be looking for to determine the strength of your own identity.

Let's consider some of the things you might look at to give you a clue to your sense of self.

Do you say yes to things you do not want to do because you want to make others happy?

Although it is not a problem to sometimes choose to do things for others because it pleases them and makes them happy, to do this all the time creates a problem. If all the choices you make in life are determined by whether or not someone else is happy, then you may have a less well-defined sense of self.

> *Valerie's husband's family members ran a small business. The family was very proud of the business, and it meant a lot to them. To minimise expenses, her husband's parents would ask family members to help out with various work tasks related to the business. They all seemed to be doing this willingly. Valerie, too, was asked to help out. Earlier on, these requests were infrequent and did not involve much effort on her part. However, over time, the demands on her time increased. It reached a point where Valerie was being expected to contribute work hours about four or five days out of every week. The problem was that Valerie hated the work, was feeling exhausted because of the extra work hours she was expected to put in over and above her own job, and was overwhelmed by resentment to the point it was affecting how she felt about her husband's family members. But Valerie kept saying 'yes' whenever she was asked to help out. She didn't want to cause any problems, and her husband's parents were always so grateful. It occurred to Valerie that she had contributed to this problem. She kept saying yes when she really wanted to say no. She realised that this was a habit she had demonstrated throughout her life. She knew there had been lots of occasions in lots of different situations when she had nodded her head and said yes, but inside her head, she was screaming 'no'.*

Are you able to identify your personal strengths?

A person with a good sense of self can identify their personal strengths. Also, they have confidence in their ability to use these strengths to reach the goals they set in life. An underdeveloped sense of self can be indicated by not knowing your strengths. If you do not know your strengths, it is unlikely that you could see how you could use them to achieve your life goals.

> *Leanne had worked at a childcare centre for the last twenty years. She didn't want to do this job anymore. She felt she had less energy than was needed to care for the young children, and she didn't like the office 'politics'. However, Leanne felt like she had no choice but to continue in the position she held. She believed she had no other skills she would need in the job market. She felt like childcare was all she knew. Those closest to Leanne encouraged her to seek a different job and pointed out what they knew she would be capable of doing. But Leanne didn't believe them. She just couldn't see that an employer would be interested in her because of her work history, and she didn't feel she had the type of personality needed to promote herself at a job interview. She was unhappy in her job but thought that she probably should be grateful she had a job at all.*

Do you know what makes you happy?

Understanding the activities that you enjoy and the people you like to spend your time with can tell you a lot about yourself. We are referring here to the things in your life that you value because they allow you to relax and be happy. The more you understand these sources of happiness, the greater your sense of self.

> *Derek's wife repeatedly encouraged him to engage in social or leisure activities that would make his life more fulfilling. Derek agreed that all he had in life was work and home and that he knew that a more fulfilling life would make him happier. The trouble was that Derek just couldn't think of anything to do that would make things better. Derek's wife suggested he join a group, but he couldn't think of what type of group to join, and everything she suggested didn't seem particularly interesting to him. He thought he would benefit from doing something more active, but the thought of engaging in a sport or joining a bushwalking group just didn't hold much attraction. He knew his wife was becoming exasperated with him, but he just didn't have a clue about what would make him happy.*

Do you know what your personal values are, and do you take these values into account in the way you live?

By talking about these values, we are referring to the personal attributes that matter to you in yourself and in others. For example, you may value honesty, compassion, trustworthiness, fortitude, kindness, self-sufficiency or courage. These things will help define your sense of self. A person with a stronger self of sense would also live in a way that is consistent with these values.

> *Heather attended a climate change rally because her friend was passionate about the issue. She attended church regularly because her mother wanted her to accompany her when she went there. Heather helped raise money for cancer research because she worked with someone who did this because that person's family had been affected by cancer. She contributed in lots of ways to her community. However, Heather was not really passionate about any of the causes to which she gave her time. It wasn't that she didn't care. It was just that she did not have the same enthusiasm about these issues, and she doubted she would involve herself in them if she was not influenced by others in her life.*

Do the decisions you make reflect your own choices or those of other people?

People's decisions about what they are going to do may be based on their own choices. These people know what they want and can set goals for themselves in an effort to achieve these things. They have a stronger sense of self. Others can struggle to do this. They allow others to make choices for them and accept the direction that others provide without consideration of whether these things fit with what they want in life. Those people have a less well-developed sense of self.

> *Walter applied for a promotion at work. He did it because his wife thought he could do more than what he had been doing, and she believed he should be given the recognition he deserved for the work he undertakes. Walter also knew that his parents had always had expectations that he would achieve more than what he had done. He knew they would be proud if he obtained the promotion. However, if he was honest with himself, he didn't want the job. He didn't want the added stress. Also, the new position would take him away from the work tasks that he liked the most. But Walter applied for the promotion. He did so because the people who were important to him expected him to do so.*

We will be considering ways to improve your sense of self later in this workbook. Before doing that, it is worth considering the strength of your sense of self – your understanding of who you are and what you stand for. Having a strong sense of self will help you if you are making changes in your life.

How should I react to what is happening to me?

Before moving on and looking at ways to manage this transition in your life, it is worthwhile taking a moment to consider how you should be reacting to this period of change.

Understand the shift in priorities

Understand that all you are experiencing, all the confusion and dissatisfaction, reflects a shift in your priorities from one thing to another. Although these feelings can push you to analyse or overly analyse the meaning of it all, fundamentally, you are experiencing this type of shift.

Normalise this experience

It will help you to understand that this is a normal experience. We make these types of shifts all the time, but probably to a more minor degree with lesser impact. Interestingly, you have already dealt with major shifts in your life because these shifts occur as part of a normal developmental process. If you believe you have never felt this way before, remember adolescence! Major shifts also can occur when you leave school and start work, when you make a commitment to a romantic partner, and when you have children.

Reprioritising things is acceptable

To make it more acceptable for you to make changes in your life, it is necessary to understand that it is reasonable for you to do so. Your quality of life is important. The goal is to make the best possible choices for yourself that will likely result in improvement in your well-being.

No one is asking you to make impulsive changes without thinking through the consequences. A reasoned approach to life changes, with due regard to the likely outcomes, certainly seems like a better approach. To do this, you need to be in the right state of mind.

A way forward

So, what do you need to do, or consider doing, to make sensible changes in life? How do you cope with the stresses associated with a big life change? This workbook will take you through a variety of strategies to deal with your confusion and dissatisfaction and to improve the chances of a good outcome.

From here, we will be covering the following:

> To start, we will teach you about why you are feeling anxious and what you can do to control these feelings. This is important for those of you who are feeling anxious. Anxiety tends to make it more difficult to think clearly. It compromises our attention and concentration. Anxiety also tends to cause us to want to avoid the very things that are unsettling us, so we tend to avoid the problems in life that need to be resolved. Managing your anxiety will allow you to feel more settled and think through the possible consequences of any choices you make.

> In learning to control your anxiety, you can also learn to reduce a sense of threat that comes when faced with anxiety-provoking life changes. Understanding threat reduction and learning threat reduction techniques can help you change your reaction to this transition in life from viewing it as a crisis to seeing it as a normal developmental change.

> The workbook will also teach you to regulate your emotions. When we are stressed, we can tend to have strong emotional reactions to problems that are either not very severe or that would be more manageable if our thinking was not influenced by being emotionally upset. We will focus on teaching you not to let your emotional reaction run out of control.

> We can learn to better control our emotions by considering and adjusting the link between our emotional state and the behaviours we choose. If our emotions are stronger and more uncontrolled, we tend to do more impulsive things or choose behaviours that are more about wanting to control our emotional state than solving the problem we face. This workbook will introduce you to simple ways of managing the emotion-behaviour link.

> We will also cover ways to set reasonable expectations. This will allow you to make sensible decisions without putting too much pressure on yourself or making demands on yourself that are too severe. We will look at the language you use when you engage in self-talk that can exacerbate the pressure you feel and will cause you to try to achieve impossibly high standards or goals.

This workbook will also introduce you to the idea that the errors in thinking we all make can affect how you respond to life situations. These errors in thinking can cause us to fail to cope when things are not the way we want them to be or when we face life challenges. By clearing up your thinking, you can make more reasoned choices and your emotional state can be better managed.

This workbook will introduce simple ways you can restore your sense of self. With a greater sense of certainty about who you are and what you stand for, decisions about what direction your life should take should be easier to make.

We will also introduce a values clarification exercise to explore the way your life is now and how you would like it to be in the future. The goal here is to ensure that any change you make in your life is consistent with your values. In this way, the changes you make have the greatest potential for resulting in a good outcome.

We will finish by considering simple ways to examine a plan for your future. We will introduce you to problem-solving techniques that will help you think through the potential consequences of any life change you might make. Although we will not be telling you what specific life choices to make, we will introduce you to ways that you can examine these possible life choices to determine their likelihood of success.

Managing your anxiety

It is important to understand your anxiety reactions as they are often experienced when we are faced with the possibility of significant change in our lives. You may know that you feel anxious but you may not yet understand what is happening to you when you are feeling anxious. This can make your anxiety reactions more unsettling than they need to be. So, let's consider how your nervous system works.

What is my nervous system doing?

Your autonomic nervous system (ANS) is the part of your nervous system that drives your functioning. It regulates your heart rate and temperature and makes other adjustments that are required for you to function on a moment-by-moment basis.

Your ANS is divided into two parts: the parasympathetic nervous system and the sympathetic nervous system. Your parasympathetic nervous system is the part of your ANS that should be driving you most of the time. It makes sure everything is ticking along so that your body gets what it needs and you can function well.

Your sympathetic nervous system has a specialised function. It is your self-protection system that automatically activates when you are under threat. So, if you were crossing the road and a truck came screaming around the corner, your sympathetic nervous system would activate so that you could quickly and efficiently move out of the way of the truck and reach safety. Adrenaline would release into your system, causing your hands to shake and your heart rate to increase, but you would reach the safety of the footpath on the other side of the road, and you would be fine. Your brain would then recognise that you were safe, your sympathetic nervous system would turn off, and your parasympathetic nervous system would take over again.

Your sympathetic nervous system is attuned to your brain perceiving signs of threat. It activates when you are at risk of harm and prepares you to deal with that threat. It is an effective self-protection system when you are under threat. Unfortunately, for people who develop an overly sensitive sympathetic nervous system or for people who are facing big changes in their lives, their sympathetic nervous system can activate at the slightest indication that something is wrong and will prepare them to deal with the threat. This can occur even when there really is no threat to manage. This is what happens when you are anxious in the absence of an obvious cause of your anxiety and is the case when you are facing a life change. In effect, your brain cannot distinguish between an external threat (e.g., a truck coming around the corner) and an internal threat (e.g., you thinking worrying or anxiety-provoking thoughts). An overly sensitive nervous system will rely on its self-defence mechanism to protect you from perceived harm.

Your nervous system will also react to crises in your life that do not present the same level of physical harm as would occur if you were facing being run over by a truck. Although it is stressful to be worrying all the time, this itself is not physically threatening to you. Nevertheless, your sympathetic nervous system can be triggered by your worrying thoughts. As stated, your brain cannot always distinguish between an external threat to your physical integrity and a threat to your emotional well-being that is caused by the way you think.

Below is a table providing an overview of the activities of the parasympathetic and sympathetic nervous systems.

Table 1: The functions of the parasympathetic and sympathetic nervous systems.

	Parasympathetic	Sympathetic
Eyes	Constricts pupils	Dilates pupils
Salivary glands	Stimulates salivation	Inhibits salivation
Heart	Slows heartbeat	Accelerates heartbeat
Lungs	Constricts bronchi	Dilates bronchi
Stomach	Stimulates digestion	Inhibits digestion
Liver	Stimulates bile release	Simulates glucose release
Kidneys		Stimulates release of adrenaline and noradrenaline*
Intestines	Stimulates peristalsis and secretion	Inhibits peristalsis and secretion
Bladder	Contracts bladder	Relaxes bladder

* Also known as epinephrine and norepinephrine

When your sympathetic nervous system is activated, a series of physical changes occur that make sense if they are in response to a threat to your physical integrity. Some of these changes are listed below.

>Adrenaline is released so that you are alert and in a heightened state, ready to deal with the threat. This causes your heart rate to increase and can cause your hands, or even your whole body, to shake.

>Your hearing and your eyesight become better than normal. Everything sounds louder than it really is, and it is difficult to tolerate lots of light and movement. This

is why anxious people tend to avoid places like supermarkets. Too much noise, too much light, and too much movement can be overwhelming when you feel anxious. Anxious people tend to tolerate these things poorly because of the acuteness of their senses when their sympathetic nervous systems are activated. It helps to have really good hearing and eyesight if you are being threatened, but it does not help if you are just trying to do some shopping.

In our view, the most amazing thing that happens is that your sympathetic nervous system shuts down the systems it does not need to be using. For example, when under threat, your body needs to produce lots of glucose for energy, so it stimulates glucose production. However, other systems that are not needed are shut down. In particular, your sympathetic nervous system shuts down your gastrointestinal system (e.g., inhibits digestion and inhibits peristalsis and secretion, with peristalsis referring to the contraction of the muscles that push forward the contents of your digestive tract). This is all right if it is shut down for the period of time it takes for you to deal with a truck coming around the corner. Your body copes less well with your gastrointestinal system not functioning well if the sympathetic nervous system activation is prolonged. You can lose your appetite, experience nausea, develop diarrhoea or, less commonly, constipation, and you can experience difficulty eating, or you will overeat to try to control the uncomfortable state of your digestive system.

All of these symptoms make sense if you are under threat but become a problem if the activation of your sympathetic nervous system is prolonged. Also, when your sympathetic nervous system is activated for reasons other than obvious threat, you can develop a sense of imminent danger just because your sympathetic nervous system has taken over your functioning. When your sympathetic nervous system is activated, your brain will interpret this as a sign that something is wrong. This explains why you feel this overwhelming sense that something terrible is going to happen and your worrying thoughts increase.

Later, we will introduce you to some straightforward ways you can bring your sympathetic nervous system under better control so your anxiety and fear are reduced. You can learn to control the thoughts that are related to this confusing time of your life that may be causing you to feel as if something terrible is happening.

Range of arousal

To better understand how things work, you should be aware that human beings have a range of nervous system arousal within which we function the best. This range is quite large, from low in the range when we are very relaxed to high in the range when our nervous system is more 'revved up'. Pictured below is a diagram of this arousal range. The range within which we function best is known as the *window of tolerance*.

Within this window of tolerance, you have the flexibility to respond to the demands being placed on you. In this way, your arousal level will increase when you are faced with a demand and then decrease when that demand is over. As long as your arousal stays within this window, you will respond well to pressures placed on you.

If your arousal level drops below the lowest point of that range, you will enter a state of hypoarousal. In this state, you will feel slowed down and lethargic. Your functioning at this point will be inadequate, and your ability to respond to demands will be poor. If your arousal increases beyond the ceiling level, you will enter a state of hyperarousal. When this occurs, you can feel too aroused and can feel anxious and panicky. Your functioning will be impacted, and your ability to cope with pressures will deteriorate.

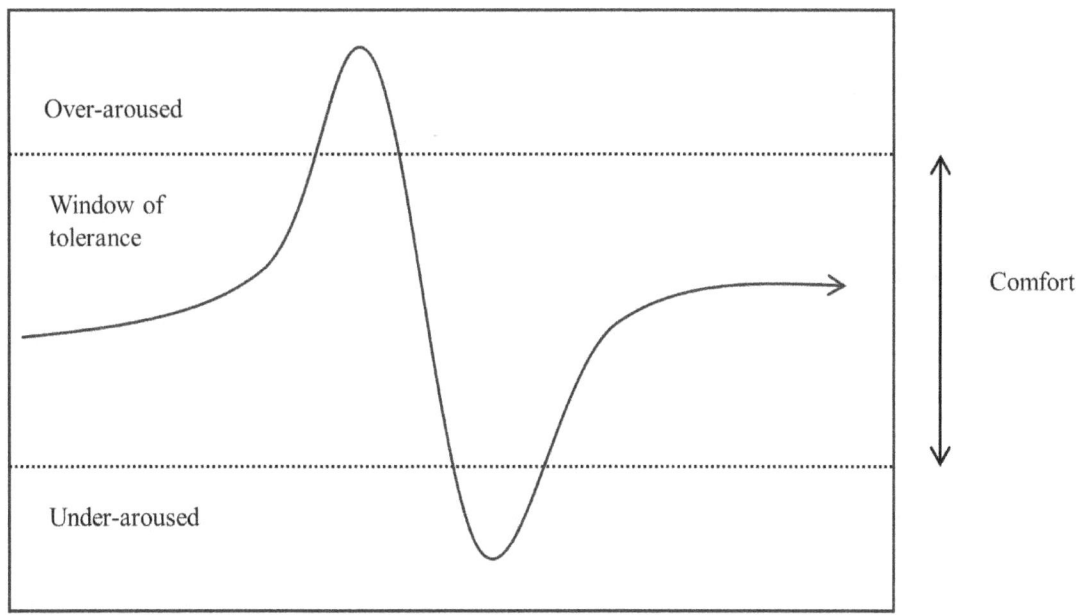

Figure 1: A diagram of the window of tolerance.

When you are confused about the situation you are in or when you are considering significant life changes and these problems are ongoing, your arousal level creeps up from an optimal level of arousal in the middle of the window of tolerance to the upper extremes. You will find that you cannot or do not reduce that high level of arousal, even when you should be able to let go. This is why people cannot sleep well when they are under pressure. They can never relax enough for their arousal to decrease to a comfortable state. So, your 'baseline' arousal level, which is the starting point from which you respond to life demands, is high up in the range instead of midway.

So, your arousal level remains elevated. You barely notice this because it starts to feel normal to be under that much stress with your arousal level that high. But a problem exists. When any other thing occurs to which you have to respond, or the level of demand on you increases, your arousal level will increase to deal with that additional challenge. However, the starting point of your arousal level, or your baseline arousal level, is already so high that you have no room to move. Any increase in arousal will push you through the ceiling and into an uncomfortable and unpleasant hyperaroused state. You will experience intense anxiety as a result.

Your high starting point gives you no flexibility to respond or react to even minor additional stressors or an increase in worry or confusion about what to do with your life. So, the ways you normally cope with demanding situations fail because you have moved out of the range where you can successfully apply your usual coping strategies.

Your goal should be to get your nervous system back under control. Having faced this period of threatened change in your life and experiencing all of the worry this entails, your arousal level gets pushed to the upper limits of your window of tolerance. Any extra demands, even minor ones, then cause your arousal level to move beyond the ceiling of the window of tolerance and uncomfortable and unpleasant anxiety symptoms are then experienced.

You need to aim to bring your optimal arousal level down to at least the middle of the window of tolerance, with a baseline or starting point, when you are at your most relaxed, to the lower end of that range. Remembering that it now feels almost normal to have your nervous system so 'revved up', you need to retrain your nervous system to have a better starting point and a better optimal arousal level.

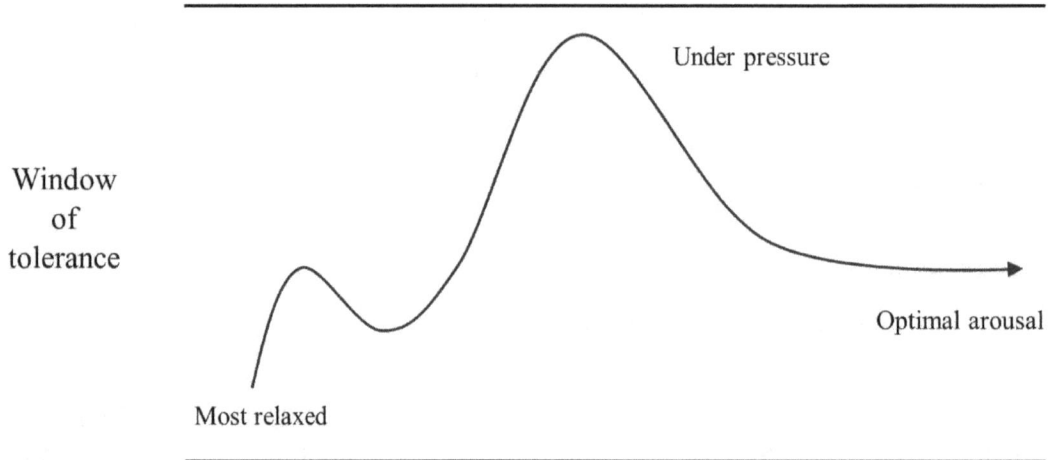

Figure 2: A diagram of an optimal level of arousal.

We will introduce you to way to control your anxiety. These use a variety of techniques. You can try them all but then you can choose the ones that best suit you and give you the greatest degree of nervous system control.

How to combat anxiety

How do you achieve anxiety management? Consider the following. When you are in an elevated or heightened state, at the top of your window of tolerance or beyond it, your heart rate increases and your breathing changes. Your heart rate elevation is caused by a release of adrenaline that occurs when your sympathetic nervous system is triggered. This can be very uncomfortable, and it feels like there is very little you can do about it.

Your breathing changes contribute to the elevation in your heart rate. When people are stressed, their breathing tends to be rapid and shallow. You can liken this pattern of breathing to the waves on top of the water. Form a picture in your mind of the way a child draws waves. When you are stressed, you will tend to breathe in sharply, then breathe out quickly and then breathe in again quickly. You tend not to breathe all the way out before you breathe in again. This inhalation-exhalation pattern is what affects your heart rate.

In contrast, when you are relaxed, your breathing tends to be deeper and slower and has a pattern that is similar to the swell in the ocean. The inhalation-exhalation pattern is a comfortable breath-in followed by a long, slower breath-out. You do not breathe in again until you have breathed all the way out.

From the diagram below, you can see the pattern of anxious, rapid and shallow breathing on the top. Below that is the pattern of slower, deeper breathing that is characteristic of a more relaxed state.

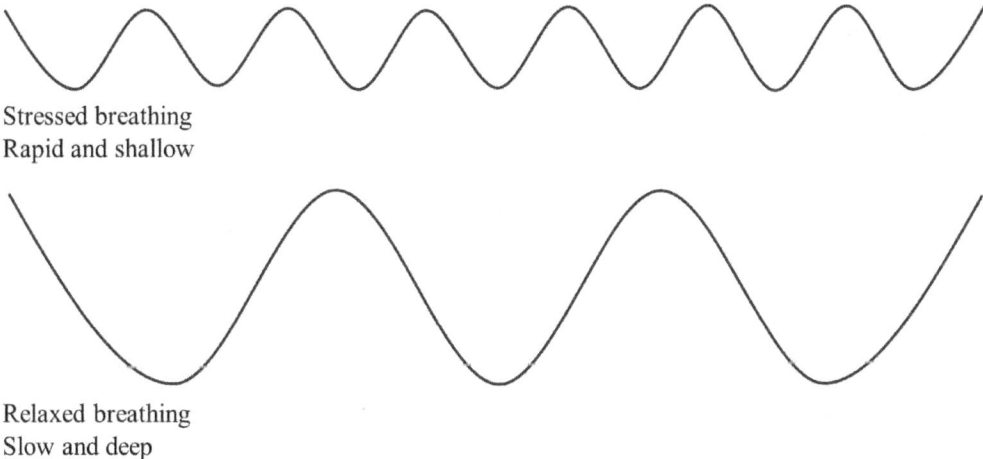

Figure 3: A comparison between stressed and relaxed breathing.

The reason your breathing pattern affects your heart rate is because these two things are linked. Under normal, stress-free conditions, your heart rate increases as you breathe in and then slows as you breathe out. This is normal. When you are stressed and your respiration rate increases and your breathing is shallower, your heart rate does not have a chance to slow before you breathe in again. Therefore, your heart rate is elevated and stays up.

Let's, for a moment, go back to the truck speeding around the corner, threatening to run you over. Your sympathetic nervous system is activated, allowing you to be in the right physical state to move quickly out of harm's way and protect yourself. When you get to the other side of the road, the truck goes past, and you are unharmed; your brain registers these experiences, your sympathetic nervous system turns off, and your parasympathetic nervous system takes over. This is because reaching the other side of the road and seeing the truck pass you by are safety signals. Your brain interprets these signs as indicators that you are going to be all right.

Of course, no such safety signals are available when you are going over in your mind your dilemma about the direction your life should take. This is not the sort of event that allows for a safety signal. Your brain would struggle to identify safety indicators because they do not exist in that sort of form. What you can do is offer your brain a safety signal but of a different type.

You can send a message that everything is all right by deliberately slowing your heart rate from its elevated rate to a more normal rate for you. Although it sounds difficult to achieve, controlling your heart rate is actually a reasonably straightforward undertaking. If you slow your breathing and lengthen your exhalation until you have breathed all the way out before breathing back in, your heart rate will come into line with your respiration rate, and your heart rate will go down.

To use our waves and ocean swell analogy, the aim is to change the pattern of your breathing from waves on the top of the water to a pattern like the swell in the ocean, where the water is lifted up and then put back down as the swell passes. You are aiming for an easy, comfortable breath in, followed by a long, slow breath out.

The ideal situation is to breathe out for twice as long as it takes you to breathe in. Lengthening your breath out requires that you slow the amount of air you breathe out so that you can breathe out for longer. You should aim to breathe all the way out, emptying your lungs, before you gently and comfortably breathe back in.

This pattern of breathing should result in a slowed heart rate and a subsequent reduction in that sense of anxiety or crisis that occurs when your sympathetic nervous system is triggered. This occurs because your brain interprets the reduction in heart rate and the change in breathing pattern as a signal that the crisis is over.

Let's consider a simple exercise to control your breathing by deepening your breaths and slowing them down.

	Slowing and controlling your breathing
1.	Without trying to change your breathing, just notice for a moment the pattern of your inhalations and exhalations.
2.	Now, take a comfortable breath in. It does not have to be too deep, rather just a comfortable breath.
3.	Now, breathe out, slowing the amount of air you exhale and lengthening your breath as a result.
4.	When your lungs feel empty of air, gently and comfortably breathe back in.
5.	As you breathe, practice lengthening your exhalation just a bit. You may also deepen your breath in slightly. Keep in mind the picture of the ocean swell if this helps.
6.	Practice this pattern of breathing for as long as you feel comfortable.

Exercise available at elemen.com.au

There is another element that you can add to this breathing exercise that may help with your ultimate goal of reducing your anxiety and signalling your sympathetic nervous system to turn off so your parasympathetic nervous system can do its job. You can include in this breathing exercise the element of reducing your muscle tension.

People who are stressed tend to have tense muscles. Although this muscle tension can occur anywhere in the body, common sites include the forehead and scalp, neck, jaw, shoulders, and chest. The increased muscle tension contributes to the overall sense of readiness to deal with threat. On the downside, tense muscles can cause headaches, chest and other pain.

If tense muscles present a significant problem for you, then a progressive muscle relaxation exercise may help. A general overview of this technique is provided below. More comprehensive versions are available online. However, another easy strategy is to link the relaxation of muscles with the breathing exercise.

As you breathe out, just relax your muscles in places where they feel tight and tense. You do not have to achieve marked muscle relaxation to experience a noticeable difference. Just drop your shoulders, relax your jaw, smooth your forehead or relax your stomach muscles. Aim for a gentle relaxation of tight muscles as you exhale.

The combination of breathing exercise and muscle relaxation can be used even when the focus is on controlling your breathing. You can also use the combined technique when your primary focus is on troubling muscle tension. In combination, the techniques can help with either target.

	Combined breathing and muscle relaxation technique
1.	Take a comfortable breath in. It does not have to be too deep, but rather just a comfortable breath.
2.	Now, breathe out, slowing the amount of air you exhale and lengthening your breath as a result. As you breathe out, drop your shoulders, relax your jaw, smooth your forehead and relax your abdominal muscles.
3.	When your lungs feel empty of air, gently and comfortably breathe back in.
4.	As you breathe, practice lengthening your exhalation just a bit. You may also deepen your breath in slightly. Keep in mind the picture of the ocean swell if this helps. Continue to relax your muscles slightly on each exhalation.
5.	Practice this pattern of breathing and muscle relaxation for as long as you feel comfortable.

Exercise available at elemen.com.au

As stated, if muscle tension presents you with a significant problem, you may wish to try a method of progressive muscle relaxation. This technique involves tensing your muscles and then relaxing them. Tensing your muscles before relaxing them has a number of purposes. It helps you to clearly identify where the tension in your body is located. It helps you feel the difference between a tense muscle and a relaxed one, which is helpful when the muscle has been tense for a long time. Finally, tensing the muscle first helps to induce deeper relaxation in that muscle when you relax it.

We will start with a longer version of the progressive muscle relaxation exercise that will help you learn the technique. You can then change to a shorter version that we describe below.

	Progressive muscle relaxation (longer version)
1.	Choose a comfortable place where it is quiet. Lay down or sit in a comfortable position with your feet flat on the floor.
2.	Now, clench both your fists… tighter and tighter. Notice the tension in your muscles. Keep them clenched for about 10 seconds. Now relax. Feel your muscles relax. Notice the difference between the tension and relaxation.
3.	Repeat the procedure with your fists. Notice the difference between tension and relaxation.

4.	Now, bend your elbows on both arms and tense your biceps. Hold the tension. Now relax. Notice the difference between tension and relaxation.
5.	Repeat the procedure with your elbows bent and your biceps tensed. Hold the tension, then relax. Pay attention to the change from tension to relaxation.
6.	Now, frown as hard as you can. Notice the tension in your forehead. Hold the tension. Now relax. Notice the difference you feel after you have released the tension.
7.	Now, frown again as hard as you can. Hold the tension, then release it. Notice the contrast between tension and relaxation.
8.	Now, close your eyes and squint them tightly. Hold the tension then relax. Allow your eyes to feel a comfortable relaxed state. Notice the change. Repeat by closing your eyes and squinting then relaxing, letting go of the tension.
9.	Now, clench your jaw. Bite down hard. Notice the tension throughout your jaw. Now, relax your jaw, allowing your teeth to fall apart slightly. Notice the feeling of relaxation. Repeat this exercise with your jaw.
10.	Now, press your tongue hard against the roof of your mouth. Hold it there. Feel the tension at the back of your mouth. Now relax. Notice the difference between the tension and relaxation. Repeat the exercise with your tongue.
11.	Now, purse your lips, pushing them out into an 'O' shape. Hold them there. Now release the tension and relax. Notice how your mouth feels now that it is relaxed. Repeat the exercise with your lips.
12.	Now, press your head back as far as it will comfortably go. Hold onto the tension. Roll your head from the right to the left, allowing the focus of the tension to change. Now relax. Feel the difference between the tension in your neck and the relaxation. Repeat the exercise by pressing your head back.
13.	Now, bring your head forward with your chin on your chest. Feel the tension in your throat and the back of your neck. Hold the tension, then relax and allow your head to return to a comfortable position. Repeat the exercise by bringing your head forward.

14.	Now, shrug your shoulders, bringing your shoulders up and allowing your head to hunch down between them. Hold the tension. Now relax and notice the difference between tension and relaxation.
15.	Now, breathe in deeply and hold your breathe. Hold it. Now allow yourself to gently exhale, letting go of tension as you breathe out. Feel your body relax. Repeat the exercise, breathing in then gently letting go.
16.	Now, tense your stomach muscles. Hold onto the tension. Now relax. Let your stomach muscles relax and appreciate that feeling. Repeat the exercise with your stomach muscles.
17.	Now, arch your back without straining. Hold onto the tension. Now let it go. Notice the change in your muscles. Now repeat the exercise by arching your back.
18.	Now, tighten your buttocks and thighs. Press down on your heels to flex your thigh muscles. Hold onto the tension. Now relax and notice the difference. Repeat the exercise.
19.	Now, curl your toes downward to cause your calves to tense. Hold onto the tension. Now relax. Repeat the exercise.
20.	Now, draw your toes upward, causing your shins to feel tense. Pay attention to the tension. Now relax. Repeat the exercise.
21.	Now, scan your body. Notice if there are any tense spots. Repeat the exercise in that area.
22.	Enjoy the more relaxed feeling throughout your entire body. When you are ready, slowly return to your normal activities, holding on to that feeling of relaxation.

Exercise available at elemen.com.au

Once you have learned the technique, you can use a shorter version. You may prefer to just focus on the areas of your body that are particularly tense. It is certainly the case that some people tend to carry their muscle tension in one or two areas. Here is a shorter version that will allow you to tailor the procedure to suit your own needs.

	Relaxing using progressive muscle relaxation (short version)
1.	Choose a comfortable place where it is quiet. Lay down or sit in a comfortable position with your feet flat on the floor.
2.	Begin to work your way through groups of muscles by tensing them and relaxing them. For example, if you start with your forehead, tighten the muscles in your forehead by frowning. Hold for a few moments (10-15 seconds), then release, allowing the muscle in your forehead to relax, enjoying that experience for about 60 seconds. Notice the difference between the tension and the relaxation.
3.	Then, move on to the next group of muscles. You can work through groups of muscles from the top of your head to the tips of your toes, or you can select areas of your body that present a particular problem of tension for you.
4.	Repeat the process until you have worked your way through the groups of muscles you have selected.
5.	Repeat that process again, first tensing the muscles, holding that tension for five to ten seconds, and then relaxing those muscles.

Exercise available at elemen.com.au

So, controlling your breathing and, thus, lowering your heart rate will help you feel less anxious, as will reducing your muscle tension. However, there are other approaches you can take to anxiety management.

More exercises to help

One of the problems with being anxious and 'revved up' is that your mind fills up with anxiety-provoking thoughts. This is the basis of stress and worry. When you are focused on trying to make sense of what is happening to you, you cannot seem to stop thinking in an endless stream of anxiety-provoking thoughts. This makes it very difficult to get your nervous system back under control. The thoughts racing through your mind do not allow you to relax. So, included here are some exercises that should help you settle your mind.

The first exercise aims to teach you to self-soothe. If you can learn to settle yourself, the racing thoughts in your mind may follow. The quieter your nervous system, the less active your mind is with anxiety-provoking thoughts.

What you are aiming to do is find ways to soothe yourself. Most of us can understand how we go about soothing an upset child. We might hold and rock a distressed child and say soothing things. What you are looking for are adult versions of self-soothing strategies that will help to alleviate your distressed state.

The goal of developing self-soothing strategies is to create for yourself some moments of less distress. The strategies are aimed at reducing your heightened state to a more manageable level. They allow your nervous system arousal level to be brought back under your control. So, strategies that allow you to focus on the here and now are the ones that will allow you to choose to be in a quieter state with a greater sense of peace of mind.

Consider the proposed self-soothing strategies listed below and select ones that you think might assist you. These may be things you have tried before or ones you feel might work for you. Some of these strategies require you to make an effort to seek out the means of engaging with them. However, others are using things that are readily available or easily obtained.

	Self-soothing strategies
1.	Take a shower or a warm bath. Focus your attention on the sensations created by the water. Enjoy the feeling of the water on your skin and the warmth of the water.
2.	Play with your pet, or just stroke your dog's or cat's coat. Interacting with your pet has been demonstrated to be soothing for many pet owners.
3.	Change into your most comfortable clothes. Enjoy the feel of the fabric and the degree of comfort you feel from wearing these items of clothing.
4.	Go for a swim. Enjoy the sensation of being in the water. Allow those sensations to quiet your mind. Even if you are not a good swimmer, bobbing around in the water can produce the same sensations.
5.	Treat yourself to a massage if that appeals to you. Allow your muscles to relax and your mind to quiet.
6.	Listen to soothing music. Allow your attention to be directed to the music rather than have the music in the background.
7.	Listen to an audiobook, even if your distress makes it difficult to concentrate. Try to pay attention to each word that is spoken. If you lose track of the story, you can always return to the previous track and pick up the story again.
8.	Turn on the television or talkback radio and engage in listening to what is being broadcast. The goal here is to focus your attention on the conversations as they play out rather than selecting a programme you are excited to watch or listen to. It is the process of listening to others talking that is soothing.

9.	Listen to the sounds of water running. Again, the aim is to listen to the sounds of the water, stopping your mind from going to other intrusive thoughts. You can find the sound of running water in various places. You can visit a naturally occurring water course or waterfall. You could listen to running water from an outdoor garden fountain. However, you can also get an indoor personal fountain that can be used at any time. Alternatively, you can listen to recorded sounds of water running.
10.	Find something soothing to look at. This might be by the water or an outdoor space such as a park. It could be photographs or paintings that you find soothing or relaxing. The goal is to find something to look at that is engaging for you, and that you find relaxing and soothing.

Exercise available at elemen.com.au

Managing anxiety-related thoughts

Before considering ways to change your thinking from being focused on trying to make sense of what is happening to you, it is worth mentioning here some straightforward strategies for managing the sense of threat that anxious arousal causes. Although focusing on managing the physical manifestations of anxiety and focusing on quieting your nervous system can assist you, there is also value in quieting your anxious mind.

Simple threat reduction strategy

To start, there is a simple strategy that can help quiet a stressed mind that is repeatedly going over thoughts about what is happening to you. People who are facing this dilemma tend to cast their minds into the future, trying to decide what to do. Too little attention is paid to the present. The anxiety you feel about the future destroys any peace of mind you might be able to have in the present.

Threat reduction strategy	
The strategy involves the following easy steps:	
1.	Catch yourself thinking stressful thoughts.
2.	Evaluate your immediate environment for any signs of threat.
3.	Ask yourself if there is anything you need to do right now in relation to the thing you are focusing on in your thoughts.
4.	Give yourself permission to let go of your anxiety and concern for the time being.

Exercise available at elemen.com.au

Exercises in quieting your mind

There are strategies available for quieting your mind. Building on the notion of self-soothing, it is a good idea to be more present in your focus. If you give it some consideration, you will find that the thoughts racing through your mind when you are anxious typically are not related to what is happening in the here and now. Our thoughts tend to be time-travelling, that is, they are focused either on what has already happened or what is to come. You rarely focus on what is happening in the present moment when you are trying to relax and get your worries under control.

Usually, at these times, nothing is happening that is worth being concerned about. If you could deliberately spend more time focused on the here and now and less time on the past or future, you would have a better chance of relaxing and quieting your overly stimulated nervous system.

The notion of focusing on the here and now is based on mindfulness techniques. Mindfulness refers to your ability to be aware of your emotions, your physical state, your actions and your thoughts in a state of mind that is absent from judgment or criticism of your experience. Research has demonstrated that mindfulness helps you to control symptoms of anxiety, to control the distress caused by particular situations, to increase your capacity to relax, and to learn how to cope better with challenging situations.

Based on the notion of mindfulness, we have included some exercises you can use to quiet your mind by focusing on the here and now. To do this well, you may need to practice the skill. When you first learn these techniques, it is easy to become distracted and return to your racing thoughts. Do not worry if this happens. Just return to your exercise and continue.

Mindful listening	
1.	Sit in a comfortable place, preferably by yourself. If you wish, close your eyes.
2.	Start to focus your attention on the sounds around you.
3.	Notice the changes in the sounds from moment to moment.
4.	Notice the times between sounds when it is quiet.
5.	Focus your attention both on what is happening inside and outside.
6.	Pay attention to the sounds and nothing else. Do not make judgments about the sounds. Just acknowledge the sound then listen to the next one.
7.	If thoughts about other things come into your mind, put them to one side then return to listening to the sounds around you.
8.	Do this for a few minutes or until you are ready to stop.

Exercise available at elemen.com.au

Let's try another mindfulness exercise.

Mindful use of your senses	
Sight	Look around you. Allow your attention to be drawn to five things in your immediate environment that you might not normally pay any attention to. For example, this might be the way the fruit is sitting in the fruit bowl, or the way your curtain is hanging, or the way your books are placed on your bookcase. Allow your attention to rest on each of these things. Keep your focus directed at the item, setting aside any other thoughts that come into your mind.
Touch	Bring your attention to four things you can feel at this moment in time. For example, it may be the feel of the sun on your skin, or the feel of the fabric of your clothes against your skin, or the feel of the chair underneath you, or the feel of the table surface where your hand is resting. Allow your attention to rest on each of these feelings. Keep your focus directed at each sense of touch, setting aside any other thoughts that come into your mind.

Hearing	Listen to the sounds in your surroundings. Notice three things you can hear. For example, you might hear the sounds of cars travelling along the road, or the noise of the refrigerator, or the sound of the wind in the trees. Focus your attention on each of these sounds. If other thoughts come into your mind, let those thoughts go and return to focusing on the sounds you can hear.
Smell	Pay attention and search for two things you can smell. For example, you might be able to smell whatever you are cooking, the scent of plants in your garden, or the sea air if you live near the water. Keep your attention focused on each of these smells. If other distracting thoughts come into your mind, let these thoughts go and return to focusing on the things you can smell.
Taste	When you are eating, focus your attention on the tastes you are experiencing. For example, take a sip of your coffee and notice the taste. Bite into your sandwich and notice the flavours. Really pay attention to the flavours of the things you are tasting. If you become distracted, let go of these interfering thoughts and return to focusing on the things you are tasting.

Exercise available at elemen.com.au

And there is one last mindfulness exercise.

	Mindful walking
1.	As you are about to start your walk, stand still for a moment. Sense the weight on your feet as you stand there. Feel how your muscles are supporting you and maintaining your stability and balance. Be aware of your arms in a comfortable position of your choice (e.g., by your side or hands clasped, either at the front or at your back). Allow yourself to stand there, relaxed but alert.
2.	Begin to walk. Choose a comfortable pace, not too fast and not too slow. Pay attention to how your feet and legs feel (e.g., their heaviness or lightness, the energy, or even any pain). The way your legs and feet feel will form the focus of your attention. If you become distracted, return to focusing on your legs and feet.
3.	Pay attention to the way in which you lift your feet and place them back down on the surface on which you are walking. Notice how you lift your foot, swing your leg and place your foot down again ahead of where you were a moment before. Walk in a natural and relaxed manner. Move your arms in a way that feels normal for you.

4.	It is likely that your mind will wander as you walk along. Your attention will be drawn to what is around you or thoughts that come into your mind. Acknowledge that you have been distracted and return to focusing on the process of walking… the lifting of your foot, the swing of your leg and the placement of your foot in front of you. Just gently return your attention to the sensations of walking.
5.	You might focus on a point ahead of you. Focus on the steps you take as you move towards that point. One step at a time. Experience fully the sensations of walking.
6.	Keep walking mindfully until you reach your destination or the point where you decide to turn around and mindfully walk back to where you started.

Exercise available at elemen.com.au

These types of strategies can help deal with the anxiety that is triggered by facing changes in your life. However, anxiety is only one of a range of emotions you can experience when you are dealing with the possibility of change in your life. When you feel overwhelmed by what is happening at this stage of your life, you are likely to be experiencing a range of emotions, with one emotion response tending to trigger another… and another. We need to consider ways to regulate your emotions.

Regulating your emotions

Building on the skills you have learned to manage your anxiety, it is worthwhile to spend some time learning about ways to control your emotional reactions to stressful events. This will help you achieve acceptance of your situation, allowing you to feel more settled and less distressed. It helps you reduce the intensity of the emotions you feel in reaction to this unsettled time when you are contemplating making changes in your life.

Primary and secondary emotions

Emotions are the reactions you have to the things that happen to you or the things you think about. When something good is happening, you will feel pleasurable emotions, and you will respond positively to your situation. When something bad is happening, you will experience distressing emotions, and you will view your situation negatively.

Human beings can experience a full range of emotional responses, from strongly negative to strongly positive. We are complex creatures with the capacity to experience a range of emotions as a result of any one event. Sometimes, this can be overwhelming. It then makes sense to be able to regulate your emotions so that the emotional state you are in does not overwhelm you.

Let's consider how we react emotionally. Initially, when something happens, we experience an emotional response. These initial responses are referred to as *primary emotions*. They are the reaction we have to our experiences.

However, as we are complex individuals, we can then develop an emotional reaction to our initial emotional reaction. These emotions are referred to as *secondary emotions*. Secondary emotions are the feelings we have about our feelings. Let's consider an example. You are travelling in a car with a friend, and you are listening to the news on the radio. A sad news item comes on, and you unexpectedly burst into tears. Then, you feel embarrassed that you felt so sad and cried in front of your friend. The sadness you felt about the news item was your primary emotion. It was your initial reaction to what was happening. The embarrassment you felt was your secondary emotion. This was the feeling you had in response to your primary emotion.

Our secondary emotions can become quite complex. Consider the following example.

Example of complex emotions	
What happened?	*I tried to explain to my partner why I was feeling so dissatisfied with my job.*
How did you feel?	*I felt anxious (primary emotion).*
How did you react to the anxiety?	*I didn't like feeling anxious, and I wanted that feeling to go away. My anxiety made it harder for me to explain what I was trying to say.*
What do you say to yourself?	*"I am mucking this up."* *"I should be able to make it clear what has been going on."* *"I am hopeless. I should be able to say what is on my mind."*
What did you feel then?	*I felt self-critical (secondary emotion).*
How did you react to the self-criticism?	*I didn't like the feeling, and I wanted it to go away. The feeling of self-criticism wasn't helping at all.*
What did you say to yourself?	*"I am so stupid. Why can't I just say what is on my mind."* *"If I can't explain myself, then my partner will not understand how important this is to me."* *"Get a grip and stop being so ridiculous."*
What did you feel then?	*I felt angry (secondary emotion).*
How did you react to this feeling?	*I felt uncomfortable and stressed.*
What did you say to yourself?	*"I shouldn't feel angry because there is nothing to feel angry about."* *"I have created this problem, so there is no justification for feeling angry."*
What did you feel then?	*I felt sad (secondary emotion).*

So, instead of just feeling anxious, you now feel anxious, self-critical, angry and sad. Your primary emotion is anxiety, and all the rest are secondary emotions.

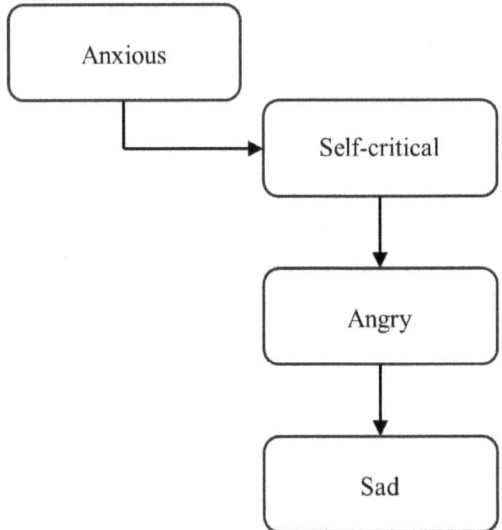

Figure 4: Diagram of primary emotion leading to secondary emotions.

One way to stop this process is to focus your attention and coping efforts on your presenting emotional state. For example, if you feel anxious then give this emotion your attention and work on ways to cope with your anxiety. The anxiety you are feeling is your primary emotion at that time. It is the emotion you feel directly because of what you are facing.

Your emotional reactions can be difficult to manage because what started as a straightforward emotional response to a stressful event turns into a confusing array of emotions. Sometimes, these emotions can compete with each other and pull you in different directions. For example, you can feel both sad and angry or angry and excited. Trying to deal with one of these emotions can be undermined by your efforts to deal with the other emotion.

Recognising and dealing with your emotions

There is a need to simplify things when you are dealing with difficult situations. You can learn to focus on your primary emotions as they arise and adopt strategies to deal with them. Let's start by looking at a way to identify your emotions so you know to what you should be giving your attention.

> *What happened?*
>> Here, consider the situation that developed that resulted in you feeling these strong emotions.

Why did this situation occur?

> Consider the possible causes of the problem situation. This is an important step. It gives you the opportunity to interpret the meaning of the problem situation in an effort to help you understand why you are feeling the strong emotions you are experiencing.

How were you feeling as a result of that situation?

> Try to identify your primary emotional response to the situation and then consider the secondary emotions you experienced as well.

What is it that you wanted to do *as a result of how you were feeling?*

> Here we are referring to the urges or impulses you have to act in response to the emotional state you are in. When feeling strong emotions, people tend to experience urges to do more extreme actions.

> It does not follow that the person will always do these things. However, thoughts about doing them can be present. It is worth noting that people tend to *think* about doing extreme things much more often than they ever *do* them. What this means is that you control the impulse to act in an 'over the top' way. If you can control these impulses, you can control others in a way that will allow you to have a more settled and reasonable response to provoking situations.

What did you actually do *and* say?

> Here, you are considering what you actually did rather than what you had an urge to do.

After experiencing those emotions and actions, how did they affect you?

> Here, we are referring to the consequences for you of experiencing those strong emotional states and your reactions to those states by choosing to act in a particular way.

Let's start by taking the process of experiencing an emotional reaction a step at a time. Let's consider the idea you have to explain to your partner why you are dissatisfied with your job.

Understanding your emotions worksheet - example
Time and date: *Thursday, 10th.*
What happened? *I had to have a discussion with my partner about my dissatisfaction with my job. The discussion didn't go as I had planned and I ended up becoming upset.*
Why did this situation occur? *There are a few reasons I was in this situation. Firstly, things had got so bad at work that I could no longer ignore what was happening. I needed to talk to my partner about what I was experiencing. Secondly, I needed to tell my partner because this was something that would have an effect on the whole family if I decided to leave my job. Finally, I didn't explain myself very well because it wasn't clear in my own mind why I was feeling this way about my job.*
How were you feeling as a result of that situation? *I felt really anxious about telling my partner* (primary emotion) *and having to explain why I was no longer happy in my job. Then, when I messed it up and didn't explain myself very well, I felt really stupid and self-critical* (secondary emotion) *because I should have been able to make it clear what I was experiencing. I then felt really angry* (secondary emotion), *not only because I had messed it up but because I then made myself feel worse than I would have otherwise if I had just been able to explain myself well. The fact that I was angry with myself then just made me feel sad* (secondary emotion).
What is it that you wanted to do as a result of how you were feeling? *I wanted to never have to go to work again and never tell anyone that I had quit my job.*
What did you actually do and say? *I just reminded myself there was nothing to feel anxious about. My partner has always been supportive of me and I would expect the same support with this problem I am facing. I reminded myself that the fact that I couldn't explain myself properly is because I don't understand the situation myself which is exactly the reason I wanted to discuss it with my partner. I then explained to my partner that I was struggling to describe what was going on because I was confused myself.*

After experiencing those emotions and actions, how did they affect you?

In the beginning, I felt like the problem was so big that it would never be solved. But, after I dealt with my anxiety by reminding myself that I have a supportive partner who would want to help me with my confusion about the situation, I felt much more settled, and we were able to talk through what had been going on.

To try and make sense of what you are feeling and why you are feeling it, we suggest you use the worksheet below. It is designed to help you to understand how you are reacting to the problems you are facing and this may direct you to how you can cope with the situation.

Understanding your emotions worksheet
Time and date:
What happened?
Why did this situation occur?
How were you feeling as a result of that situation?
What is it that you wanted to do as a result of how you were feeling?

> What did you actually do and say?
>
> After experiencing those emotions and actions, how did they affect you?

Worksheet available at elemen.com.au

Remember, here, your goal is to focus your attention on your primary emotion. If you can resolve your primary reaction to the problem you are facing, then other secondary emotions may either not occur or simply resolve. When you experience secondary emotions, tell yourself that you are going to focus your energy on your primary emotional reaction. You can then give your attention to finding ways to cope with the triggering source of your distress.

Does the size of your emotion fit your problem?

In addition to the complexity of primary and secondary emotions, there is another factor that you should consider. Sometimes, we experience a strong emotion that is inconsistent with the size of the problem. That is, we might feel furious in response to a minor provocation when slightly annoyed would probably do the job. Let's examine this idea by first considering the range of emotions you might experience.

When you think about the range of emotions human beings experience, it can seem like an overwhelming number of feelings that would form an endless list if you decided to write them all down. To make sense of people's experience of emotions, there have been lots of complex conceptualisations developed of the types of emotions we experience.

Although it is interesting reading to learn of theorists' different views about our emotions, we are going to simplify the matter for the purpose of learning to regulate your emotional states. It is worth considering that, although we do have lots of emotional states, they tend to fall into four categories. These categories are as follows:

Glad

Mad

Sad

Bad

It is pretty much the case that any emotion you can think of would fall into one of these four categories. Let's take a moment to consider this. Below are some examples of the types of emotions that would fall into each category.

Table 2: Examples of emotions in each emotion category.

Emotion category	Examples of emotions
Glad	Happy, excited, joyful, content.
Mad	Annoyed, angry, furious, hostile.
Sad	Despondent, unhappy, miserable, forlorn.
Bad	Ashamed, disgusted, horrified, frightened.

When we examine the range of emotions we are capable of experiencing, it is apparent that some of these emotional states within each category are milder, and some are more intense or severe. When trying to make sense of your emotions, a good place to start is to put the emotions you are feeling into the appropriate category and to also consider the intensity of the emotion you are feeling. For example, in the sad category, you might be feeling mildly unhappy, or you might be feeling quite miserable. In the mad category, there is clearly a difference between feeling annoyed and feeling furious.

There is one other thing you need to consider. We can develop a habit of experiencing severe or intense emotions when a milder emotion would be sufficient for the demands of the situation. Consider this example.

> *Lucia had a habit of having angry meltdowns no matter what the severity of the provocation. Her parents said her emotions went from zero to one hundred at the drop of a hat. Her partner said he would have to walk on eggshells in case something he did triggered a major tantrum. For example, Lucia's partner had agreed to pick Lucia up after work. They agreed that he would arrive to collect her at 5 pm. However, he got stuck in traffic and did not arrive until 5.12 pm, causing Lucia to have to stand on the footpath and wait for him to arrive. Her partner knew when he saw her standing there that she was furious. Although it was not his fault, Lucia berated him on the trip home for being late. Her fury was obvious. She was clearly upset and she let him know it.*

Lucia and others in her situation have a problem. Their emotions only have one speed – flat out. So, what happens when the triggering problem is only a minor one? It does not make any sense to have an intense emotional response in reaction to a minor problem.

In general, people like to have consistency between their emotional state and their perception of their problem. When you have a strong emotional response in reaction to a minor problem you can experience what is known as cognitive dissonance. This can occur when a person holds two opposing beliefs, that is, *I am feeling something very strongly* and *This is a minor problem.*

Cognitive dissonance is an uncomfortable experience. The person will try to resolve this cognitive dissonance to bring the two opposing beliefs into line with each other. In general, this would make the person feel more comfortable. So, rather than choose a different intensity of emotion, the person will simply view the problem as bigger than it deserves to be.

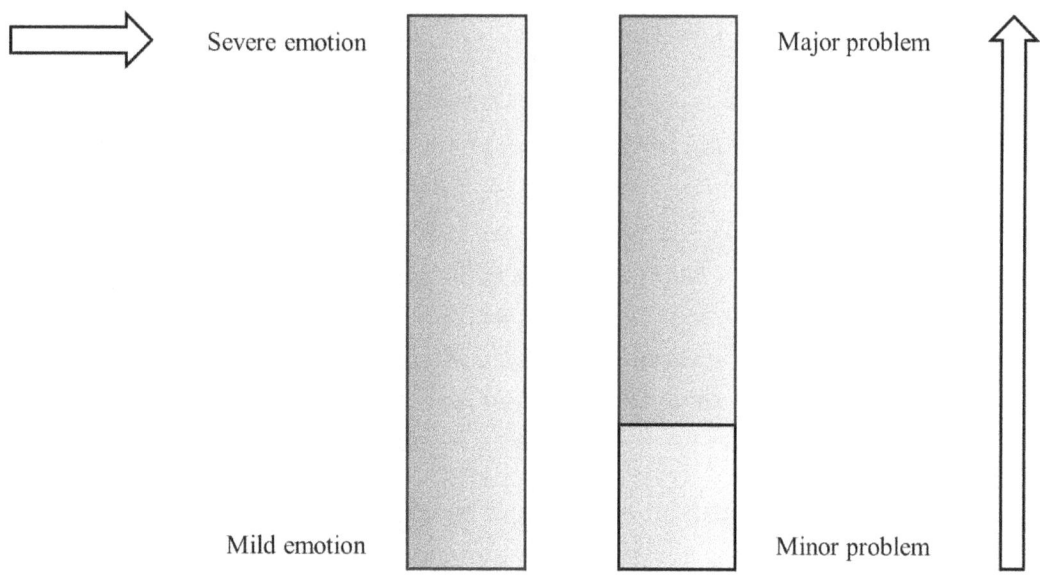

Figure 5: How cognitive dissonance causes an inflation in the perceived problem size.

From this diagram, you can see that if a person experiences the strongest emotion, they can push up the perceived severity of the problem they are experiencing to match the severity of the emotion. In our diagram, only the bottom portion of our problem column represents the actual severity of the problem. However, because the person is experiencing a severe or intense emotional response, they identify the problem as much worse than it needs to be so that their emotion and the problem match. Although you would think that experiencing the emotion and the problem at the most extreme end of the scale would make a person feel worse, interestingly, it makes them feel better because there is then no disconnect between the emotion and the problem.

Let's revisit Lucia.

> *Lucia's partner was late picking her up. He said he would be there at 5 pm, but he didn't turn up until 5.12 pm. Lucia was furious. As she became increasingly worked up, she said to herself that he should not have left her on the side of the road, waiting on the footpath. She decided this was a disrespectful thing to do. She thought he probably did this deliberately. She decided that she was not going to let him get away with this. He was going to learn never to do this again.*

Lucia turned a 12-minute wait into a major stressful life event by the way she chose to look at the situation. She did this because her strong emotional reaction was inconsistent with a minor problem, so she just made the problem seem bigger. She then felt justified in feeling furious, and any cognitive dissonance she might have felt did not emerge.

How might Lucia have reacted differently?

> *Lucia's partner was late picking her up. He said he would be there at 5 pm, but it was now after five. Lucia was tired and wanted to go home. Lucia wondered what was keeping him, but she could see that the traffic was especially heavy, and that was the likely explanation for him not being on time. Lucia realised her partner could not control the traffic, and she knew that being a few minutes later than anticipated was not a huge deal. She would be home soon enough. Lucia felt slightly irritated by having to wait, but she knew that would pass as soon as her partner arrived and she was on her way home.*

Rather than assigning the severity of the problem based on the intensity of the emotion you feel, it is better to determine the severity of the problem and then decide how much emotional energy you are going to give it. As you start to feel a strong emotion, ask yourself what is triggering it and how you are going to choose to feel in response to it.

For example, rather than being terrified about any potential change to your life, it might be better to choose to feel apprehensive. That feels like the right amount of emotion for a situation that you are figuring out how to control. Save 'terrified' for an event that actually warrants that type of reaction. Notice that apprehensive and terrified fall into the same emotion category (bad) but are on opposite ends of a scale from minor to severe.

We can look at a way to evaluate your problem size and its associated emotional state. Remember, you can examine your reactions in retrospect until you have better control of this tendency to make small problems bigger than they need to be. Use the following worksheet to examine how you reacted to an event and how you might have viewed things differently. Consider the following example.

Problem size worksheet - Example
What happened? *I realised I needed to talk to my partner about some changes I might make in my life.*
How did I feel about this at the time? *I felt so anxious, I couldn't sleep. I was dreading having a conversation about what was going on for me. I felt sick at the thought of having the discussion.*
Rate the intensity of this feeling   Mild| 1   2   3   4   5   6   7   **8**   9   10 |Severe
What was I telling myself? *I was thinking that, by talking to my partner, I was committing myself to going ahead with major changes in my life. I thought that if I started talking about what I was thinking there would be no turning back. I thought my life was going to change in lots of ways that I could not control.*
Rate the perceived severity of the problem   Minor| 1   2   3   4   5   6   7   **8**   9   10 |Serious
How could I have looked at this problem differently? *I should have realised that talking about something with my partner didn't commit me to anything. There is nothing frightening about having a conversation with my partner about what I had been thinking. In fact, I would welcome the input. A discussion with my partner would have made me feel less alone in my thoughts and less anxious.*
Rate the severity of this problem from this new perspective.   Minor| **1**   2   3   4   5   6   7   8   9   10 |Serious
What intensity of emotion should I give to this problem now?   Mild| **1**   2   3   4   5   6   7   8   9   10 |Severe

Below is a copy of the worksheet that you can use to examine how you should be reacting to problem situations that arise.

Problem size worksheet
What happened?
How did I feel about this at the time?
Rate the intensity of this feeling   Mild| 1   2   3   4   5   6   7   8   9   10 |Severe
What was I telling myself?
Rate the perceived severity of the problem   Minor| 1   2   3   4   5   6   7   8   9   10 |Serious
How could I have looked at this problem differently?
Rate the severity of this problem from this new perspective.   Minor| 1   2   3   4   5   6   7   8   9   10 |Serious
What intensity of emotion should I give to this problem now?   Mild| 1   2   3   4   5   6   7   8   9   10 |Severe

Worksheet available at elemen.com.au

The importance of understanding this relationship between emotion and problem size is because there is also a strong link between our emotional state and how we choose to behave. Strong, negative emotional states can drive us to behave in ways that we might not behave if we were not feeling so out of control emotionally. By learning to control our emotions, it makes it easier to behave in ways that benefit us rather than make the situation worse.

The link between emotions and behaviour

When you are experiencing discontent in your life, and you are facing potential changes, you can feel strong emotions. This can be a difficult and uncomfortable time. It would be helpful for you to be able to manage those strong emotions.

This does not mean that you should fight against the emotions you feel. You cannot start a war with your emotional state and expect to be the victor. However, you cannot ignore your emotions and expect them to just disappear. The aim should be to recognise and validate your emotional reactions but do what you can to avoid your emotional distress escalating.

It is worthwhile to understand the link between your emotional state and the things you choose to do in response to that emotion. This is important. It is difficult to control your behaviour choices if you do not appreciate the link between how you feel and what you do.

Let's consider how you might behave in relation to your emotional responses. Consider this example.

Imagine that you have experienced an argument with family members about you wanting them to do more so that you have more time for yourself. They were reluctant to agree and argued that they were busy and didn't have time to do more than they already were doing. You argued that they were being selfish.	
I felt	What I did
Angry	*I became increasingly infuriated with them and told them their attitude was terrible. I raised my voice and shouted. I called them selfish and labelled them as horrible people. I stormed out of the room and slammed the door. I then refused to talk to any of them.*

Understanding this link between your emotional state and your behaviour can help you learn to make different choices in how you act when you are upset. Let's consider here how you might opt to do things differently. Consider the same example but now let's look at how this person might have chosen to behave in an alternative way.

I felt…	What I did	What I could have done instead
Angry	*I became increasingly infuriated with them and told them their attitude was terrible. I raised my voice and shouted. I called them selfish and labelled them as horrible people. I stormed out of the room and slammed the door. I then refused to talk to any of them.*	*I could have stayed calm and explained to them why I had been feeling so overburdened. I could have explained that I would take account of their existing commitments when asking them to take on some tasks. I could have asked for some input from them about ways they saw that I could deal with my problem.*

Let's take this one step further and consider the likely outcomes of the initial behaviour choice and the alternative one.

I felt	*Angry*
I did…	*I became increasingly infuriated with them and told them their attitude was terrible. I raised my voice and shouted. I called them selfish and labelled them as horrible people. I stormed out of the room and slammed the door. I then refused to talk to any of them.*
What happened?	*I continued to feel angry and upset. The atmosphere in the house was very uncomfortable, and everyone was upset. I found it difficult to find a way back to re-establishing our normal relationships.*
A better choice…	*I could have stayed calm and explained to them why I had been feeling so overburdened. I could have explained that I would take account of their existing commitments when asking them to take on some tasks. I could have asked for some input from them about ways they saw that I could deal with my problem.*
Likely outcome…	*I might have been irritated that they didn't initially agree to my plan but, by keeping the conversation going, I could have given a good argument for why I needed things to change. I could have worked out a plan with them that met all our needs.*

Initially, you can work on thinking up alternative and healthier behaviours after the event. This will allow you to learn how to make better choices by considering the different outcomes of various behaviours. It will then become easier to apply this strategy at the time you are feeling the emotional reaction so that you can choose the better behaviour at the time and avoid doing things that might feel all right at the time but do not help you in the longer term. Below is a worksheet you can use.

The emotion-behaviour link worksheet
I feel/felt…
I did/I felt the urge to do…
What happened/what would have happened?
A better choice…
Likely outcome…

Worksheet available at elemen.com.au

You will feel better if your emotional state is more under your control. This does not protect you from strong emotions, but it allows you to handle them in manageable ways. This can help you reach a point where you can deal with this transition period in your life in a way that is comfortable and manageable for you.

However, to do this, you might need to adjust your expectations. We often have a particular view of how things can work out. We set rules for ourselves that we feel we must follow. Perhaps you need to consider whether the rules you set for yourself and the expectations you have of how things should be are working for you.

Setting reasonable expectations

In an upcoming section, we will be focusing more on how your thinking can affect how you feel and the choices you make about what you are going to do about the problems in life you face. Here, we want to introduce you to the idea that the rules you set for yourself can influence how you feel. Also, we will consider how you can enforce those rules in ways that make things more stressful for you rather than less stressful.

Setting expectations

The expectations you set for yourself can be unreasonable. You can hold the mistaken assumption that if you just try hard enough, you will be able to cope with whatever comes your way. So, you just push yourself harder and harder, expecting that you will cope. We want to talk about the rules you set for yourself and your expectation you will be able to live by those rules.

There are two features of the expectations you can set for yourself that will present you with problems. Firstly, it is easy to set expectations and standards for your behaviour that would exceed most people's capacity to cope. The rules you set for yourself may include aspects such as 'I should do everything I set out to do', 'I should do everything properly and well', and 'I have to follow through and complete everything I set out to do.

Secondly, these rules you make tend to be set in stone. That is, no matter what is happening in your life, you believe that you have to rigidly adhere to these rules. You can believe this to be true even if the situation you find yourself in is different than you have ever experienced before or your current situation is making you very unhappy. You can believe it to be true even if you also hold the view that others should have the right to make changes in their lives and should do so if that is what they want. After all, we are all quite capable of having a different set of rules for ourselves than we have for others. We expect ourselves to cope when we are more sympathetic towards others in the same situation.

In an effort to start to bring your situation under control, you must consider the expectations you are setting for yourself. The rules you set need to be flexible so that you can adjust when the demands on you fluctuate. Below are some commonsense reminders you might like to consider.

Table 3: Commonsense reminders for when you are setting expectations.

1.	You have every right to change your mind. If your circumstances change or your views on a matter change, you can reject earlier decisions and choices in favour of more current and appropriate ones.
2.	Decisions you made at earlier stages of your life may no longer be appropriate for you at your current stage of life. It is reasonable to change your perspective as you move through your life.
3.	You cannot be expected to have known things you did not know when you made earlier life choices. We gain wisdom as we move through life, and it is reasonable to apply that wisdom to the decisions we make about our current situation and our future.
4.	Everyone has a limit. You cannot be expected to persevere in an unsatisfactory situation if alternative options are available to you.
5.	Even if you feel stuck in your current situation, it is possible to explore opportunities, consider different potential outcomes and make different choices that will make you feel more in control of your life.

Before moving on to examine your thinking and how this might be affecting your situation, we need to consider one other factor in relation to expectations. This relates to a simple mistake that people make that tends to increase how overwhelmed you feel rather than relieve it.

Language you use when talking to yourself

One of the problems that you can create for yourself is that stressful things happening in your life can feel worse because of the way you talk to yourself about your experiences. The expectations you set can feel more exaggerated because of the way you view them.

In particular, we are all capable of making demands on ourselves, even when they do not exist. When we talk to ourselves, we say things like "I must do this" and "I should do that" or "I have to do what I set out to do". Everyone does this and, usually, it does not have any really noticeable effect on how we are feeling. However, when we feel stressed or overwhelmed, talking like this exacerbates the stress we are feeling.

Consider the example below of Annette.

> *Annette was standing in her kitchen, holding a cup of coffee while she looked out the window. It was early, and she had some time to spare, and she was thinking about her day. She knew she had to do two things that day, and she didn't want to do either. She really didn't want to do them. She was supposed to turn up to a local charitable organisation and help sort out items that had been donated. She had been doing this for some time, and although she had been happy to help, there were now two people who were regularly there and who weren't pleasant to be around. But she said she would help, so she told herself she must go and do what she said she would do. Then she said she would attend an afternoon tea party being held by a friend of a friend. The thought of attending the afternoon get-together was so unappealing that she just couldn't wait for it to be over. Although she didn't want to attend, she knew she should go because she said she would accompany her friend. Annette sighed. She was not looking forward to her day. She realised that today was the same as many of her days. It was full of things she didn't want to do, but she knew she would do it because she said she would. She had to do what she said she would do. Annette knew she had to get on with her day, but she was reluctant to move away from the window.*

Annette's self-talk was full of 'must', 'should' and 'have to'. With language like that going through her mind, everything seemed like a pressure. We all do this. We feel like things are imperative, so we make demands of ourselves. Even without really noticing, we speak to ourselves in ways that exacerbate our stress. It makes us feel that we have no choice, and this perceived lack of choice is stressful in itself.

But, is this really true? It is actually the case that you could lay on the grass and look at the sky all day long if that is what you chose to do. Of course, you probably would not do that but you absolutely could do that if you chose to do that.

In fact, most, if not all, of what we do is a choice we make. We may feel some pressure to do things or to act in a particular way, but the way we act is based on decisions we make for ourselves. We take into account all of the information available to us at the time, and then we make a decision about what we are going to do.

Are you unsure this is true? Think about it. How many times have you acted in a particular way or undertaken a particular task because it suits you to do that, even if the task you undertake is not a preferred one? Consider the following comments.

> I will do it to get it out of the way.

> I will do it so she stops nagging me about it.

> I will make a dental appointment even though I hate the dentist because I want to make sure my teeth are healthy.

> If I get the housework out of the way, the rest of the day is mine to do what I want.

> I would rather do the job myself than leave it to my colleague.

> It is easier to pick up after the children than to keep growling at them.

You can probably generate a long list of similar comments you make to yourself. All reflect the choices we make and the decisions we reach. These choices generally have good underlying rationales. We make these choices and decisions because, in some way, they work for us.

Then why do we keep talking to ourselves like things are imperative and the demands are real? There are probably numerous reasons. We might do it because it has become a habit. We might do it because it feels like it is true. We might do it because of the stress we feel. But what would happen if you stopped making these demands and, instead, expressed them as preferences in a way that is genuinely the case?

Reframe your expectations in terms of preferences, not demands

To alleviate the additional stress that is caused by using demanding language, you might like to try changing the way you speak to yourself. To start understanding how to do this, let's revisit Annette's thoughts from early morning.

> *Annette was standing in her kitchen, holding a cup of coffee while she looked out the window. It was early, and she had some time to spare, and she was thinking about her day. She thought about what was in her diary for the day. Today was the day she volunteered at the local charitable organisation. It wasn't as much fun as it used to be, primarily because of a couple of people who were unpleasant to be around. Annette thought she would go today because she would not feel comfortable letting people down at the last minute. However, she decided that she would start looking around for other avenues to help out in the community. Volunteering was a choice Annette had made, but she realised she could also choose where she volunteered. She felt all right about her decision to offer her services elsewhere. Annette remembered that she had agreed to attend an afternoon tea party being held by a friend of a friend. She knew that the party wasn't something she was interested in, but she had wanted to support her friend who had asked her to attend. Annette felt her support of her friend was more important than a couple of hours doing something that didn't particularly interest her. Annette put down her coffee cup. She decided she would make a start on her day.*

Do not underestimate the additional stress you can feel from wording things in a demanding way. It is a good idea to practice changing your demanding internal self-talk into a statement of preference. Consider the following examples.

Reframing demanding self-talk - examples	
Demand	Preference
I must cook dinner.	*I think I will get on and cook dinner; otherwise, I will end up with a house full of hungry people... including me.*
I have to do all those jobs at work that have been piling up.	*I think I will clear all those jobs that have been piling up. It will feel good not to have them hanging over my head.*
I have to go do some gardening for an elderly neighbour.	*I will choose to do some gardening for my elderly neighbour because she cannot do it herself and her tidy garden makes her happy.*
I shouldn't take time away from the family by doing things for myself.	*I have chosen to devote my time to my family but I know it is all right to balance up what I do for the family with what I do for myself.*

Below is a worksheet you can use. Catch yourself making demands and reframe them as a statement of preference.

Reframing demanding self-talk	
Demand	Preference

Worksheet available at elemen.com.au

It is evident that what we say to ourselves can affect how we feel. Now, we need to consider other ways our self-talk can influence how we feel and what we do.

Changing your thinking to manage your mood

To feel better, you might have to change the way you view the circumstances in your life in an effort to alter the way you react to them. Certain ways of thinking tend to make us feel more distressed, more vulnerable and more overwhelmed than we need to feel. The goal is to challenge this type of unhelpful thinking so that it can be replaced with the type of thinking that is a more accurate reflection of your situation. Let's consider ways you can challenge unhelpful thinking and replace it with the types of thoughts that allow you to see things more clearly and choose behaviours that will help you.

How are our thoughts affected?

As we go through life, we can develop unhelpful thinking styles or errors in our thinking. These errors influence how we interpret the world around us and how we fit into that world. It an attempt to make sense of the world, we develop 'templates' or models of how we think things should work.

For example, you might develop a template that tells you that you have to be the best at everything you do. On the surface, this seems workable. You may just have to work hard and keep things in your control. However, if you have a template that you *have* to be the best, what happens when you have too much to do and too little time to do it, or things influence your performance that are out of your control? You then become upset with yourself. You feel like you are not good enough, even in situations where you tried your hardest to succeed. We have met lots of people who want to succeed, but because of factors outside their control, they have been unable to achieve the standard of perfection they set. This could be you. Unfortunately, your template tells you that to be 'good enough', you *must* be the best in all areas of your life, that you must function at 100% capacity no matter what, and that if you do not do something perfectly, you have failed. You can see the problem.

Our individual templates are put together based on information from a variety of sources, including, for example, our personality and our experiences throughout life. If the messages we receive from our experiences in life are good and healthy ones, we tend to have good and healthy templates of how the world works and how we fit into that world. However, if the messages are distorted in some way (e.g., being told you have to be the best at everything you do, that no one will like you if you disagree with them, your needs are not as important as other people's needs), then the template we develop will reflect these messages and will be unhelpful.

Core beliefs

So, how does this template affect us? It tells us how we should respond when dealing with our world and the people in it. The information we gather determines our 'core beliefs' about three things:

> How safe or dangerous we perceive the world to be.
>
> Our place in that world and our value as a person.
>
> How certain the future feels.

These core beliefs are not the 'truth' of things. They develop as a result of the information we gather along the way in life, whether or not that information is helpful or unhelpful, clear or confusing, or accurate or distorted.

If we have helpful, clear and accurate templates, then our core beliefs are healthy, and our thinking does not contain errors about how the world works and how we fit into that world. However, if we have unhelpful, confusing and distorted templates, our thinking contains errors that affect how we react to the world and how we view ourselves in that world.

Cognitive errors

Cognitive errors are the errors in thinking that occur when our templates of how the world works and how we fit into that world send us the wrong message. Our thinking about our experiences is then altered by the wrong message. Problems arise when we engage in certain types of cognitive errors.

Below are some of the most common cognitive errors. As you read through them, think about whether these types of errors occur in your thinking.

Table 4: Descriptions of the common errors in thinking.

Types of errors in thinking	
Error type	*Error in thinking*
Filtering	A person whose thinking is affected by filtering takes the negative details of an event and exaggerates them while filtering out any positive aspects of the situation. For example, you might believe you are stuck in your current situation because you are not capable of finding a way forward despite having a history of solving your life problems.

Polarised thinking	With polarised thinking, things are either 'black or white' or 'all or nothing'. People who think this way place situations in 'either/or' categories, with no middle ground to account for the complexity of most situations. For example, you might think that you have only two choices – either you completely change absolutely all aspects of your life, or you will continue to be miserable.
Overgeneralisation	A person makes a conclusion based on one event or a single piece of information. In this way, if something bad happens to them on one occasion, they expect it to happen over and over again. For example, you might think that because you once left a good job for one that did not work out as well as you expected, that any change of job would work out poorly.
Jumping to conclusions	If a person jumps to conclusions, they 'know' what the other person is thinking about without that person saying so. For example, you might feel sure that other people would believe you are selfish if you took some time for yourself.
Catastrophising	A person who catastrophises expects disaster to strike, no matter what. A person hears about a problem and uses *what-if* questions to imagine the worst outcome. For example, you might believe that if you choose to take your life in a different direction, bad things will happen that you would not be able to avoid.
Personalisation	A person believes that everything others do or say is some kind of direct, personal reaction to them. They take everything personally. For example, you might interpret someone's comments about how devoted they are to their career as a criticism of your confusion and uncertainty about yours.
Control fallacies	This occurs when a person strongly endorses the view that there should be control in all situations. This can occur in two ways. Firstly, there is external control where the person feels they are a helpless victim of fate or, secondly, internal control where a person assumes responsibility for the pain and unhappiness of others. For example, you might feel your situation in life was inevitable and cannot be changed because of your life circumstances and history.

Fallacy of fairness	A person who believes they know what is fair will feel resentful and unhappy if others disagree with them. People who judge every event in their lives in terms of whether or not it is fair will often feel resentful, angry and hopeless. For example, you might feel resentful because you have given up so much to support others without others making changes to give you what you need and want.
Blaming	This person holds other people responsible for their own emotional pain. Alternatively, they may blame themselves for every problem – even those clearly outside their control. For example, you may hold your partner responsible for your unhappiness with your life situation because they seem happy with theirs and they took advantage of opportunities offered to them.
Shoulds	Should (must, have to) statements (e.g., I should visit my parents more) are made by people who hold rigid rules about how the world should work and how everyone should behave. Breaking these rules makes a person angry. They also feel guilty when they violate their own rules. For example, you might tell yourself you must continue on the same path your life is on because of the responsibilities you feel you cannot avoid or the expectations of others.
Emotional reasoning	People with this distortion in thinking are guided by what they 'feel' is the truth. They will rely on their feelings to establish whether or not something is 'fact'. If a person feels stupid and boring, then they must be stupid and boring. Emotional reasoning blocks rationality and logic. For example, you may believe that all the choices you have made in life have been bad ones just because your current situation is making you unhappy.
Fallacy of change	A person with this type of thinking will believe that if they apply enough pressure, others will change to meet their needs. This person needs others to change because they cannot cope if others disagree with them or behave in ways that are contrary to how this person feels they should behave. For example, you might believe that all of your immediate family members should change to meet your current and changing needs even though their lives are satisfactory for them.

Global labelling	A person generalises a small number of features or characteristics of themselves or others and inflates them into a global statement or judgment. This goes beyond overgeneralising. Rather than take into account the context of a situation, the person will apply this judgment to all aspects of a person or situation. For example, you might label yourself as 'hopeless' just because you are struggling to cope at the moment.
Always being right	When a person engages in this error of thinking, they insist that all views held by them or actions done by them are correct. In their view, they cannot make a mistake or be misinformed. For example, you might insist on changes to your relationship because you feel discontented in life rather than because there is evidence of relationship problems just to prove a point.
Heaven's reward fallacy	A person who engages in this type of thinking believes that a person's hard work and sacrifice will pay off in the end, as if someone is keeping track of what everyone does in life. Sharing some similarities with the fallacy of fairness thinking, this person believes that the one who does the most or, works the hardest or sacrifices the most will be the person who is rewarded at some point in the future. For example, you might believe that if you continue on an unrewarding path because it benefits others, there will come a day when good things will come your way. You just have to be patient.

Let's consider how these errors in thinking affect a person's point of view. Below are examples of these types of logical errors in thinking, along with a more rational point of view.

Table 5: Examples of rational and irrational perspectives for each error in thinking.

Correcting your thinking	
Error in thinking	*A rational view*
Filtering	
Joel had another bad day at work. He attended a meeting where his views were ignored, and Joel believed that changes would be made that would be detrimental to his team. Joel wanted to change jobs. This was just another example of why he did not want to work for this organisation anymore. But Joel felt stuck. He believed that because he did not immediately have another job opportunity, he was stuck in this job. He had changed jobs before but now he had financial responsibilities so he felt he could not just walk away from his current job. He felt hopeless and did not know what to do. He thought this was just too big a problem from him to handle.	In reality, Joel had a good history of coping with life problems. He also had a good history of job seeking and successful transition to a different job. However, because of his current situation, Joel was ignoring all of this information and focusing only on his current situation. Further, because he had not been heard at one meeting, Joel believed that any attempt to be heard would be ignored. He filtered out information that would highlight that he had always worked effectively as a team leader. Joel would have been better off focusing on his skills and his history of coping with transitions and changes in his work life so he could develop a plan for a way forward. This would have been better than just doing nothing and feeling overwhelmed.

Polarised thinking	
Stuart knew that things had to change. He was unhappy, and his mood was affecting all aspects of his life. He believed that the only way to change this was to 'fix' everything in his life. Although he felt overwhelmed, Stuart started to make a list of the things he needed to do. He put on his list his need to change jobs, move house, end his relationship with his long-term partner, find new friends, distance himself from some family members who were causing him some anguish, and engage in activities that would make him feel physically stronger and more powerful. The list was overwhelming, but he thought he had to do these things, or he was just going to continue to feel miserable.	Stuart was making the mistake of assuming that 'everything' was to blame for the unhappiness he was feeling. Without even considering whether or not various aspects of his life were satisfactory or not, he decided to conduct a complete overhaul of his life. Stuart would have been better off giving more consideration to the contribution of various aspects of his life to properly evaluate the extent to which these things were responsible for his unhappiness. The last thing Stuart needed to do was 'throw the baby out with the bathwater' and get rid of or change the parts of his life that were actually fine. If he could narrow his focus and identify the areas that were actually causing him to feel unsettled, his task of changing those things would be less daunting than a complete life overhaul.

Overgeneralisation

Sophie hated her job. She was underpaid for the amount of work she was required to undertake. She had to work long hours to complete her workload, and her bosses thought nothing of contacting her outside of her working hours. She felt like she had no private life as a consequence. She did not particularly like her colleagues and, although she realised she did not have to be friends with them, she really had to force herself to be civil when working with them. She did not respect her bosses, who tended to expect her and others to do the bulk of the work while they were often absent from the workplace. However, Sophie was reluctant to resign and look for another job. The decision to leave another job for the one she was in now did not work out very well for her. In retrospect, Sophie believed that her previous job was better than the one she had now. Sophie thought that if she changed jobs again, things would work out the same. She believed she would end up being even more unhappy than she was now. She was coming to believe that there was no such thing as a good job.	Although it is the case that Sophie's decision to change jobs ended up with her being unhappy, there was no reason to assume that any decision to change jobs again would turn out the same. Sophie assumed that one bad outcome somehow indicated that all outcomes would be bad. Sophie would have been better off considering the aspects of her current job that were contributing to her unhappiness and then choosing a future position that did not have these characteristics… at least to the best of her knowledge. For example, she might want to seek a job that did not involve an unrealistic workload or outside of work hours demands. She might want to choose another job where she could work more independently and be adequately paid. Certainly, there is nothing about one poor outcome that would determine all outcomes in the future.

Jumping to conclusions

Rebecca's boss asked her to take on a special project in addition to her normal day-to-day workload. This special project required her to learn new skills. There was no one in the organisation who could teach her these skills so she had to look to other sources on the Internet to learn how to do what was being asked of her. This made the task very difficult. Her manager was understanding of the demands being placed on her and had expressed his gratitude for her efforts.

Rebecca was exhausted. Having to take on the special project, learn the skills she needed and do her normal duties was too much. However, Rebecca was reluctant to take any time off or to take any time away from the normal demands of her life at home. She did not ask for help. Rebecca believed that if she took time off or asked for help at home, her manager and colleagues and her family at home would consider her to be selfish and lazy.

Rebecca made the mistake of jumping to the conclusion that others would view her need to look after herself and find ways to cope with the overload she was experiencing as evidence of selfishness and laziness. Although Rebecca would have been pressed to give evidence of why she held this view, given statements of understanding she had received, she believed with a good degree of certainty that this was how people would view her. Rebecca would have been better off communicating her needs to her manager and her family members and then allowing them to express their own views about her need to look after herself rather than assuming that they would hold a particular point of view.

Catastrophising	
Patricia wanted to sell their current home and move to a different area away from the city. It had been her husband who loved living in the city and Patricia had tolerated it until recently. Now she yearned to live in a quiet country community. She wanted to be away from the hustle and bustle of the city. She wanted to really get to know her neighbours and be involved in her community. However, despite strongly desiring this change, she did not dare take that step. Although she had discussed it with her husband and he had agreed that it was a good time in their lives to move away from the city, Patricia was worried that her husband would either leave her or his feelings about having to make a change he had not ever really wanted would change his feelings for her and damage their relationship.	Obviously, Patricia was faced with an important decision that would have an impact on their day-to-day lives. Certainly, the decision was a big one, and the outcome was likely to have a significant effect on them. However, Patricia made the mistake of assuming that terrible things would happen if she did what she wanted to do. Patricia would have been better off looking at the information she had available to her before predicting a catastrophic outcome. Her husband said he supported her idea of moving out of the city. She rejected that statement of support because of her anxiety rather than because there was evidence that what he was saying was not correct. At best, she would have to say that she did not know what would happen, but she would do her best to improve the chances of a good outcome from her decision.
Personalisation	
Julia was having a chat with a friend. Her friend was talking about her own experiences in her work life. She was talking about how satisfying it was to have a professional role that involved helping others. She talked about her work as meaningful. Her friend indicated that she could not be happier with the career choice she had made. Julia had been questioning her own career choice and had been unhappy about her job and was dissatisfied. So, she interpreted her friend's comments as a criticism of Julia's own choices. She felt hurt by her friend's 'attack'.	Julia made the assumption that the comments being made by her friend about her own career were somehow intended to be a reflection of Julia's situation. Julia would have been better off realising that two things can be true at the same time without them being related. That is, it was most likely to be true that Julia was unhappy with her job, *and* her friend was happy with her career choice.

Control fallacies	
On reflection, there was a list of things that Ben had wanted in life that he did not have and, he believed, would never have available to him. He had always wanted to work in marine biology, but his life circumstances had made it difficult for him to seek further education. His family situation had been difficult, and he sought a job straight out of school to help support his family financially. He had always wanted to travel the world and see all the exciting things different places had to offer. However, the job Ben had did not pay well enough for him to travel. He wanted to achieve things that made a difference in the world, but he ended up doing what he considered to be menial work. Ben felt that his path in life was determined by things that were not in his control. He was not born into a wealthy family, his childhood was not problem-free, and he had been given fewer opportunities than other people. He felt he had been given no choice but to have a life like the one he had currently.	Ben had fallen into the trap of thinking that only if he had a life that was entirely different and one with greater advantage would his life have turned out differently. Ben needed to understand that he could determine the direction of his life rather than being directed by circumstance. He could seek opportunities or make things happen, even if the easiest route was not available to him. The only thing stopping Ben from doing more of what he wanted in life was his own belief that he was facing immovable barriers and rigid limits.

Fallacy of fairness

Early on in her relationship with her husband, Ruth happily agreed to the plan that she would work while her partner studied to obtain a higher education degree. She understood, at the time, that this would benefit them both because her husband would be able to secure highly paid employment. After her husband started working, Ruth made the decision to give up her job and raise their children. It was a choice she made at the time because this was what she wanted and what she thought would be best for their family.

As time passed, Ruth became increasingly resentful. She thought it was unfair that her husband and her children had reaped all the benefits of her sacrifices, whereas she had missed out on so much. She thought it was unfair that she did not have a career or a more interesting life than the one she had experienced. Ruth's husband was confused by Ruth's anger and resentment. He believed that she had willingly made the choices, so he could not see why she was consumed by resentment about the unfairness of how her life had turned out.

Ruth made the mistake of believing that the choices she made were in the form of sacrifices that would somehow need to be repaid. Her resentment was based on the fact that she felt she had missed out while others had benefited from the choices she made. It would have helped Ruth to recognise that the choices she made in life were the ones she wanted to make at the time. Although she may want something more now, the choices she made were satisfactory for her at the time she made them. Ruth would have been better off realising that things are not fair or unfair. People are faced with decisions, and they make choices based on the information they have available to them at the time. Indeed, if Ruth was able to put herself back in the same situation with the same information available to her, she would make the same decisions because they were right for her at the time. The fact that, as time passed, she might have wanted more for herself had nothing to do with the 'rightness' of decisions she made or the sense of unfairness she felt.

Blaming

Maureen was not satisfied with her life. She wanted to do more interesting things and she wanted to have more excitement. She compared her 'boring' life with the lives of others she knew and thought her life seemed dull and uninteresting.

Maureen was angry with her husband. She blamed him for her uninteresting life. Throughout their time together, Maureen's husband had taken advantage of opportunities that came his way. He sought out interesting jobs, he had hobbies that challenged him, and he accepted invitations to engage in fun activities. Now, Maureen felt that he had taken advantage of all the interesting things. She felt she had not done the same because he was busy taking up all the offers that came his way. Despite the fact that her husband typically invited her to join in, she reasoned that someone had to take responsibility for all the mundane things in life. She blamed him for the fact that she had done less in her life than had he.

Maureen was mistakenly holding her husband responsible for the choices she had made. The fact that he took advantage of opportunities did not affect whether or not she did the same. Maureen would have been better off realising that she was the person in charge of what she chose to do. It was up to her to decide whether or not she wanted to do the things that seemed exciting and interesting.

Shoulds

Craig told himself that he had a strong sense of responsibility and he understood right and wrong. And he was probably right. This was a good description of him. However, Craig also had a long list of things that were not negotiable. He had developed endless rules for himself that were rigid and could not be broken.

Craig told himself that he must continue doing the job he hated because he had accepted the responsibilities of the job and people were relying on him. Craig believed that he must stay in his marriage despite the poor quality of that relationship because he had made the commitment of 'to death do us part' when he made his marriage vows. For Craig, there was no way out because his rules said he must do the things he promised to do, no matter the change of circumstances.

The problem for Craig is not that he had a list of rules to guide him through life, it was the fact that the rules were inflexible. He had trapped himself in an unwanted life situation because of the rigid rules he had set for himself. Craig would have been better off accepting that circumstances can change and it is reasonable to change one's perspective based on altered life conditions. This would allow Craig to have a greater sense of control of his life rather than less control.

Emotional reasoning	
Suzanne was not doing very well. Her life situation had changed in ways that were difficult for her. Her long-term relationship had ended and even though it was Suzanne who had ended the relationship, it was difficult nonetheless. There was talk of people being made redundant at work. Although she felt no great commitment to her job, she was anxious about the possibility of change. She found herself lying awake at night, unable to sleep because she was worrying about the changes in her life. Suzanne thought that the things happening to her must be bad because she felt anxious. She believed that if they were not bad, she would not be feeling anxious. She was convinced things were not going to work out well.	Suzanne made the mistake of believing that because she was feeling bad, what she was thinking must be true. This was despite the fact that both of the major changes in her life were not problematic in the long term. Her decision to leave the relationship allowed her to explore other opportunities. The same would be true if she had to give up a job she was not committed to. Suzanne would have been better off realising that any major changes in life can be unsettling. This unsettled feeling does not define the nature of the experience or determine the outcome. Suzanne could assign other meanings to these events, and their outcome will be determined by the way she handles them in the future. Her initial reaction to them will not determine her later acceptance.

Fallacy of change

Adrian was sick of his life. He wanted things to be different. He had worked hard and supported his family all of his adult life, and now he wanted things to change. Even though he had always encouraged his wife to stay at home and raise the children, he now pressured her to return to the workforce so that Adrian could stop work. Although she was not against getting a job, his wife reasoned that she would never be able to secure a position that would pay well enough to cover their expenses because of her lack of work history, Adrian continued to pressure her to take over the breadwinning role in the family. After encouraging his children to stay at home while they continued their university studies, Adrian was now telling them to move out and find their own way in life. They did not know what to do.

The pressure from Adrian was unrelenting. He was sure that if he pushed enough, he would get what he wanted… although he was not completely sure what he wanted to be different. His wife felt like she had not contributed enough and his children felt rejected. Adrian just kept pushing.

Adrian believed that because his needs had changed, everyone needed to change along with him. He was now upset about his life situation even though it has previously been quite satisfactory for him. He wanted things to change and was frustrated by what he saw as his family members' resistance. He mistakenly thought that he would get what he wanted if he just applied enough pressure. Adrian would have been better off working with his family to obtain a more satisfactory outcome for himself. He forgot that it was he, himself, who had changed his perspective on life and not everyone else. He was getting angry about things about which he had previously approved. Constant pressure was causing rifts that did not need to exist. Negotiation would have been a better approach.

Global labelling	
Overall, Brad had coped pretty well with life. He was usually an easy-going but hard-working person and took the normal challenges of life in his stride. However, recently Brad had been overwhelmed and stressed. He hated his job and it had become increasingly more difficult to force himself to go to his workplace every day. He was tired of the financial responsibility that came from paying for the purchase of a huge family home that he and his wife no longer needed now that their children were living independently. He was unhappy that so much of his focus was on work and too little time was devoted to the leisure activities he would have liked to explore. Brad started criticising himself. He formed the view that he was a terrible person who was letting his family down because he wanted more in his life. He labelled himself as irresponsible and blamed himself for not being able to cope with the sorts of things, like work and financial responsibilities, in the way that others seemingly coped. Overall, he saw himself as useless and worthless.	Brad had been struggling to deal with his current life situation and this had caused him to form the view that he was not a worthwhile person. Despite a history of being a responsible person who worked hard and cared for his family, the fact that he was fed up with these responsibilities was making him view himself negatively in global terms. Brad would have been better off considering that his current unhappiness was telling him that things were no longer satisfactory. This would have allowed him to explore ways of making things better for himself. Instead, he was criticising himself for feeling the way he was feeling. Viewing himself in such a negative light and expanding that view of himself beyond his current discontent was unlikely to help solve his problem and help him choose a different pathway forward.

Always being right

Ian told his wife that he was not happy. At first, she was sympathetic. However, Ian then told her that he thought it would be best if they separated and he moved out of their home. Although she was upset, Ian's wife tried to explore what he considered to be wrong with their marriage. Ian did not have an answer for her. He said he was feeling discontented, in general, and he reached the conclusion that it must be their marriage that was causing the problem.

Ian was able to identify there was lots of things about various aspects of his life that caused his dissatisfaction… except his marriage. However, he had reached the conclusion that his marriage was at fault and nothing was going to change his mind.

Ian's need to be right was causing him a problem. It was blinding him to the fact that, of all the things in his life, his marriage was the one thing that was working well. However, because he had thought that his marriage might be at fault, he was insistent that the marriage should end. Ian would have been better off stepping back from his need to be right to consider whether there might be other avenues of resolving his life dissatisfaction before making such a significant and life-changing decision. Obviously, things needed to change in Ian's life. However, it was not helpful to just assume that making one significant change was going to fix his problem. He needed to identify the nature of the problem first and then work on a solution rather than following through with this major change just because he believed he was always right.

| *Heaven's reward fallacy* |

Cleo was clearly unhappy. She was surrounded by supportive people who gave her good advice… if only she would listen. Cleo's husband was aware of how fatigued she felt and how much she wanted to leave her job. He encouraged her to leave and retire if she chose or have a break and then look for a different job if she preferred. But Cleo thought that she should contribute to their financial stability. Cleo's children encouraged her to do more things that made her happy. They pointed out they were all capable of looking after themselves, and she did not have to run around after them anymore. But Cleo did not want her children to face the burden of having to do more around the house. Cleo's parents encouraged her to put her own needs first and to engage in some activities that were of interest to Cleo that she had never had the opportunity to pursue. They argued that the time had come for Cleo to start looking after herself. But Cleo told them her time was taken up doing things for others. So, although Cleo was aware she was unhappy, she thought this was her burden to bear. She thought that one day… sometime in the future… when things had changed… it would be her turn.	The trouble with Cleo's view that all her hard work and dedication would somehow pay off in the end is that there was no one keeping a record of what she was doing. No one was keeping score. Cleo would have been better off understanding that if she wanted things to change or she wanted to exert some control of her unhappy emotional state, she needed to seek out opportunities and explore possibilities for herself. She was lucky she had the encouragement of those around her who cared for her, but she was the one who needed to take hold of her life and make things happen.

It is apparent that these types of logical errors do not make things easy for us. Quite the opposite. They lead us to misinterpret events so that we adopt a limited or negative perspective that colours how we view things, our emotional responses, and the choices of how we behave as a consequence.

Why do we think in unhelpful ways?

Why do we think in ways that are distorted and not particularly helpful? To understand why errors in thinking happen, we have to consider the theory behind cognitive behaviour therapy (CBT). According to this theory, our thinking has more than one level. This is displayed in the diagram below.

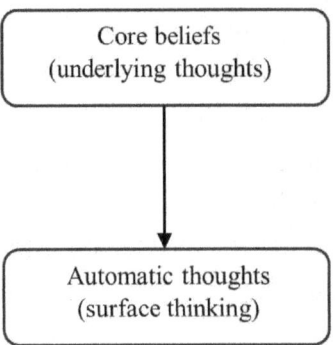

Figure 6: A diagram of the two levels of thought.

Automatic thoughts refer to the running commentary that goes through our heads as we go about our daily lives. If you pay attention, you will notice the constant chatter that goes on in your head about the things you are doing and how you are reacting to the people and events around you.

There is an easy exercise that will show you how this running commentary works. For the next minute, think about a bowl of fruit. Over the course of the minute, just let your thoughts do what they want as you think about a bowl of fruit. At the end of the minute, notice where your thoughts have taken you. Now consider the links between your starting point (thinking about a bowl of fruit) and where you ended up (thinking whatever it was you were thinking). Consider below how this might have played out for one individual. This person started thinking about a bowl of fruit and ended up thinking about a project at work they needed to complete. Follow their automatic thoughts.

> *Ok. I'm thinking about a bowl of fruit. I can picture a bowl of fruit. It's got bananas in it. I like bananas. I should buy some next time I go to the supermarket. I also need to get a loaf of bread. I must start a shopping list. Pay attention and think about a bowl of fruit. Oh, and milk, I mustn't forget milk. I hate running out of milk. Someone said once that they have orange juice on their cereal instead of milk. Yuck. I couldn't imagine anything worse. Not that I eat much cereal. I should eat more cereal... it's probably good for you. I will put cereal on my shopping list. But that might be a waste because I probably won't eat it. I have bought lots of things I thought would be good for me, but I never ate them. That reminds me that I should clean out the pantry. But I won't have the time to do that until I finish the project at work. That will probably take me another week.*

In contrast to automatic thoughts, core beliefs refer to the underlying beliefs we have about how the world works and how we fit into that world. Core beliefs have influence on our automatic thoughts. That is, we think the things on the surface in the way that we do because of our underlying beliefs about how things work. Unlike automatic thoughts, the content of our core beliefs is not readily available to us but can be examined by considering the content of our automatic thoughts.

So, where do the logical errors in thinking we have been talking about fit into this conceptualisation? Let's consider that in the diagram below.

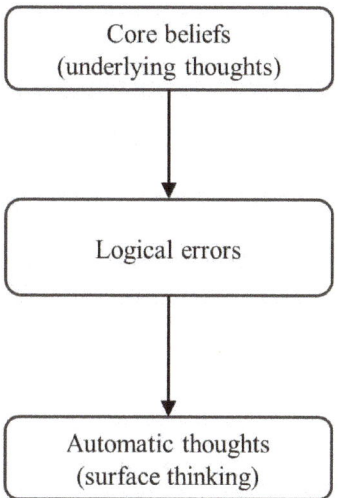

Figure 7: Where errors in thinking occur in our levels of thought.

The errors in thinking we make are a result of the core beliefs we hold. For example, if our core beliefs about the world and the future are that the world is threatening and the outlook is grim and pessimistic, then we are likely to inflate the degree of dangerousness we perceive and we are likely to catastrophise.

These logical errors then affect our surface thinking. We are more likely to be self-critical or tell ourselves everything is hopeless or tell ourselves that nothing is fair because of the logical errors we make based on our particular core beliefs.

Our core beliefs are built on the basis of a variety of influences. These include our genetic makeup (e.g., an inherited overly reactive nervous system), our experiences (the things that happen to us), the messages we receive (the things people have said to us or the way they have treated us), and the ways we have interpreted these events. If the influences are positive and healthy, our core beliefs tend to be clear, and there are few logical errors. If the influences on us are negative, unhealthy or confusing, our core beliefs tend to be inaccurate, and the logical errors we make are many and strongly influence our automatic thoughts.

Underlying assumptions of logical errors

It has been suggested that each logical error is driven by specific assumptions. If our automatic thoughts are biased, then the biases are driven by our core beliefs and assumptions. Below are some examples of cognitive errors and examples of associated assumptions. Here we are referring to the assumptions that are inevitably made if the errors in our thinking are present.

Table 6: The assumptions underlying each logical error.

Cognitive error	*Assumption*
Filtering	The only events that matter are failures. I should measure myself by my errors.
Polarised thinking	Everything is always one extreme or the other.
Overgeneralisation	If it's true in one case, it must be true in every case that is even slightly similar.
Jumping to conclusions	If it has always been true in the past, it is going to be true in the future.
Catastrophising	Always think the worst because it is most likely to happen to you.
Personalisation	I am responsible for all bad things, failures, etc.
Control fallacies	You should be able to know in advance what is going to happen. You should have seen the bad thing coming before it happened.
Fallacy of fairness	The world is a fair place, and fairness influences how things turn out.
Blaming	Whether it is me or someone else, someone is always responsible when things are not the way I want them to be.
Shoulds	People have an obligation to do specific things that cannot be avoided.
Emotional reasoning	If a person feels bad, something must be wrong.
Fallacy of change	People must change to meet other people's needs.

Global labelling	A whole person and their entire life can be summed up by a single word (e.g., stupid).
Always being right	People have to choose a side, and there is a right side and a wrong side.
Heaven's reward fallacy	Choosing to do good things for others will oblige others to do good things in return.

Let's consider how these logical errors and the assumptions that are made affect automatic thoughts. Consider in this example what this person is saying to themselves at a time in their life when they are overwhelmed by the extra demands placed on them.

Henry wanted to get out from under the burden of the obligations he felt. Some years ago, he joined a community group that focused on neighbourhood safety and enhancing community spirit. Over time, the goals of the group changed, and it was now more of an activist group that promoted particular interests by evoking community support and involvement. As the nature of the group changed, Henry's time was substantially increased by the expectations of the group. Although it was never his intention, he ended up taking on leadership roles. He couldn't say when the group changed or when his interest in the group changed, but he now wanted to end his association with the group. Henry discussed the matter with his wife.

"I have just had enough. The group is taking too much of my time... and I am not happy about some of the projects the group is taking on. Part of me... the biggest part of me... wants to just walk away and do other things with my spare time. But there is a part of me that feels uncomfortable doing that. I think that you either commit yourself to something or you don't (polarised thinking), and I said I wanted to join the group. I feel that if I walked away now, it would just prove that I am unreliable (overgeneralisation). I just know that the other group members would think I was deserting them, and they won't forgive me for that (jumping to conclusions). I worry about losing friends as a result. If the group falls apart after I leave, I will feel like it was my fault (personalisation)."

Let's break this down and see where this person is making mistakes. This person felt conflicted and made some errors as a consequence. It is a normal enough experience for people to leave a group and move on. Other people join and replace them. However, Henry was reacting to his desire to leave the group in unhelpful ways. Let's look at Henry's mistakes and their underlying assumptions.

> To start, Henry engaged in polarised thinking when he said that you either commit yourself to what you undertake or you do not. Henry holds the view that things are either one way or the other, and he discounts the important impact of changes that

occur that might influence that original commitment. In Henry's case, he failed to take into account three important facts. Firstly, the original commitment did not involve the extra hours the group activities were demanding of him. Secondly, the very nature of the group had changed so that the one he originally committed to no longer existed. Thirdly, Henry has the right to change his mind.

Next, Henry made a statement that if he left the group, he would prove himself to be unreliable. This is an overgeneralisation. Even if it was the case that Henry was behaving in an unreliable manner by leaving the group, which we would dispute is the case, his decision to leave the group did not reflect on his general reliability or his demonstration of his reliability over the course of his life.

Then, Henry jumped to conclusions about how others would react to his decision to leave. He assumed that he knew how people would react when, in fact, the best he could do was guess. It was not certain that his fellow group members would feel deserted by him or that they would never forgive him. It is unlikely that one decision on Henry's part would cause all people to hold a negative view of him forever.

Finally, Henry made the mistake of making himself responsible for the longevity of the group for some indeterminant time into the future. In truth, there could be a multitude of factors that could influence the survival of the group. It is unlikely that Henry could be held personally responsible for the failure of a group of which he was no longer a member.

The errors in Henry's thinking have made the decision about whether or not to leave the group much more difficult than it needed to be. Let's find out how to change these errors in thinking to protect yourself from the negative effects of logical errors.

Understanding automatic thoughts

Rather than thinking in positive (or negative) ways about all things, the goal here is to teach you to think in a more realistic and balanced way so that you can cope better and deal with the fact you are facing a difficult period in your life. This is done in a number of steps. Let's start this process.

Everybody experiences automatic thoughts. They reflect our way of making sense of and reacting to the world around us and to internal experiences, such as anxiety or memories and urges. Automatic thoughts are often highly believable, even when they are based on logical errors. As a result of their believability, we tend not to challenge them. If they pass unchallenged, they can have a profound and detrimental effect on our emotional state. For example, if a person believes they must please everyone all of the time, they are likely to feel bad if someone expresses displeasure or disagrees with them or in situations where they have to say no to a request being made of them.

Consider this example.

> *This person's goal is always to make sure that people are happy with what she does. She describes herself as a 'people pleaser'. However, she began thinking that there were some things she would like to do for herself that would please her. As a result, she made a plan to enrol in a weekend photography class that included a photography day trip. Her husband had work commitments on the same weekend, and she was looking forward to having time for herself to choose what she did with her time. A friend then phoned, informing her that she had plans to go away on that same weekend with her husband and asked whether she could drop her three children off to stay for the weekend. Let's examine the content of this person's self-talk.*
>
> *"I don't know what to do. I was really excited about my plans to use that weekend for my photography course. But I really should help out my friend* (shoulds). *I don't know how I will cope with her children with my husband being away as they are a bit of a handful at the best of times. But, if I say no, I will be a terrible friend* (global labelling). *If I can't go to the photography weekend, I will be disappointed, but I should be able to cope with my disappointment. It is my own fault that I made plans for the weekend without considering what other people might need* (blaming). *I suppose if I do the right thing and help my friend now, it will be my turn to get some help when I need it in the future* (Heaven's reward fallacy).*"*

It would be hard to think this way without feeling upset with yourself. We tend to believe the things we tell ourselves, even if they are not true. This person is telling herself that she had some sort of requirement to do what was asked of her by a friend despite knowing that it was not what she wanted and that she had made other plans for the weekend. Her thoughts were telling her she must agree to her friend's request, making her feel very unhappy.

Catching automatic thoughts

It is important to pay attention to your automatic thoughts so that their content can be used to identify both the logical errors you are making and, ultimately, your core beliefs. The way to go about this is to keep a thought record related to times when you notice a change in the way you are feeling.

In their simplest form, a thought record asks you to identify the event that has occurred, to take notice of the thoughts that go through your head at the time of the event, and to record the consequences you experience, both in terms of how you feel and how you might act in response. Consider the example below of a simple thought record of a mother of three who has two volunteer positions and who helps her husband in his business without being paid for her work. This person has been asked by her siblings to plan a party for their parents' wedding anniversary. She has a reputation for being the best party organiser in the family.

A	B	C
Activating event	Belief or thought	Consequence: emotional and behavioural
My brother and sister asked me to select the venue and organise a party for our parents' wedding anniversary because, they said, I throw the best parties.	*My brother and sister always go out of their way to load me up with things to do. I bet it is because they think I have more time than them because I don't have a paid job.*	*I felt so frustrated I rang them both and told them they were only doing this because they hated me.*
My family disagreed with my decision to have a theme for the party.	*They are just wrong about this. I'm not giving in on this. I will show them.*	*I felt really angry. I went ahead and ordered invitations with the theme I chose.*

We do not usually pay much deliberate attention to the fact that we are having thoughts going through our heads, even though they can have such a profound effect on how we are feeling and what we choose to do as a result of feeling that way. To change our thinking, we have to learn to identify our automatic thoughts. When we consider the events that trigger a response in us, we can usually identify what went through our mind at the time.

By keeping track of your automatic thoughts, you can learn of patterns in your thinking that are linked with particular negative feelings and the behaviours you choose because you are feeling that way. Use the simple thought record below to keep track of your automatic thoughts in relation to events that stress you.

Simple automatic thoughts worksheet		
A	B	C
Activating event	Belief or thought	Consequence: emotional and behavioural

Worksheet available at elemen.com.au

Understanding and noticing logical errors

Everyone makes logical errors. It is important to understand this point. It is when the error you are making (e.g., everything should be fair) conflicts with how things really are (e.g., the world is neither fair nor unfair; it just is the way it is) that problems arise. However, it is also important to be able to recognise the logical errors you are making so that you can correct them and correct the problems in your core beliefs. To start to do this, you can try the simple approach of expanding on your thought record form so that you include the types of logical errors that are reflected in your automatic thoughts.

Let's go back to our original thought record form and expand the examples.

Expanded thought record form - example			
A	B	C	D
Activating event	Belief or thought	Consequence: emotional and behavioural	Logical errors
My brother and sister asked me to select the venue and organise a party for our parents' wedding anniversary because, they said, I throw the best parties.	*My brother and sister always go out of their way to load me up with things to do. I bet it is because they think I have more time than them because I don't have a paid job.*	*I felt so frustrated I rang them both and told them they were only doing this because they hated me.*	*Jumping to conclusions*
My family disagreed with my decision to have a theme for the party.	*They are just wrong about this. I'm not giving in on this. I will show them.*	*I felt really angry. I went ahead and ordered invitations with the theme I chose.*	*Always being right*

Despite this person's brother and sister giving a reasonable explanation for making the request, that is, their sibling is a good party organiser, this person has jumped to the conclusions that they have a different reason for their request. In this way, this person has reached a conclusion that is unwarranted and without evidence. This has caused her to feel frustrated. She then felt driven to escalate the problem by phoning her siblings to express her unhappiness.

Against the views of all other family members, this person chose a theme for the party. This person was determined to show she was right despite this decision causing more work for her. The anger felt in response to the rejection of the theme idea triggered a determination to prove the rightness of the idea by going ahead and ordering the invitations that, in effect, forced the issue.

Below is an expanded thought record form that you can use to identify the logical errors in what you are thinking.

Expanded thought record form			
A	B	C	D
Activating event	Belief or thought	Consequence: emotional and behavioural	Logical errors

Worksheet available at elemen.com.au

Reframing your thoughts (cognitive restructuring)

The process of challenging our negative automatic thoughts is called cognitive restructuring. This is what we are trying to achieve here. The conclusions we reach because of our logical errors should be challenged and replaced with something that is healthier and more accurately reflects how the world really works.

Although there are lots of ways you can go about restructuring your thinking, we are going to introduce you to a straightforward method. We are going to start by ensuring that you understand the difference between fact and opinion. This is important as our thoughts and decision-making should be based on facts and not the opinions we form because of incorrect information that can underlie our core beliefs. For example, an opinion would be "I am stupid" (suggesting an underlying core belief of worthlessness). You might form this opinion because someone has repeatedly told you that you are stupid or because they acted in a way that encouraged you to believe you are stupid. It is not the truth or a fact that you are stupid. It is a belief you have or an opinion you have formed because of incorrect information.

We refer to the opinion on which you rely as a work of fiction. That is, you write a story in your head about what is happening and then act as if the story is true. You need to be able to identify when you are relying on the story you have written in your mind rather than basing your thoughts on factual evidence. Let's start by having a go at identifying fact from opinion or fiction. In the spaces provided, you can add other things you have been thinking and consider whether they are facts or opinions.

Fact or fiction worksheet		
Statement	*Fact*	*Fiction*
I am stupid		√
I love bushwalking	√	
I am ugly		
I forgot to renew my driver's licence		
No one likes me		
This will be a disaster		
I'm not good enough		
I feel unhappy about certain things.		
I hate my job		
I should know what is about to happen		
There are times when people feel stressed		

Worksheet available at elemen.com.au

The facts here are:

    I love bushwalking

    I forgot to renew my driver's licence

    I feel unhappy about certain things.

    I hate my job

    There are times when people feel stressed

The statements that are opinions are:

    I am stupid

    I am ugly

    No one likes me

    This will be a disaster

    I'm not good enough

    I should know what is about to happen

Why should we make this distinction between what is a fact and what is an opinion? It is because the errors in thinking we make are based on opinion and not on fact. Further, because we hold this opinion, we assume that it is true because we are thinking it and not because it is based on fact.

To tidy up our thinking and remove the logical errors, we have to rely on those thoughts that are based on fact alone. We can reject thoughts that are just based on our opinion because our opinions can be faulty. Factual information will be a good guide for us to determine whether or not we should believe what we are thinking.

Cognitive restructuring worksheet – Example
What I am thinking *My brother and sister always go out of their way to load me up with things to do. They think I have more time because I don't have a paid job.*
Facts supporting the thought *They asked me to organise the party.*
Facts contradicting the thought *They said I organise the best parties.* *I have organised good parties in the past.* *My siblings have commented before on how impressed they have been with the parties I have thrown.* *My brother and sister have told me that I work too hard and take on too much.*
Is this thought based on factual evidence or opinion? *This thought was just based on my opinion. I just thought they were picking on me because I am not working. They never said any such thing.*

By looking at the facts for and against a point of view being true, you can work out the value of holding that opinion. It seems like a waste of time to be thinking a particular thing and being negatively affected by it emotionally and behaviourally if you cannot even determine that the opinion reflects the truth. You can use the worksheet below to examine your thoughts in terms of the facts supporting what you are thinking and the facts that contradict what you are thinking.

Cognitive restructuring worksheet
What I am thinking
Facts supporting the thought
Facts contradicting the thought
Is this thought based on factual evidence or opinion?

Worksheet available at elemen.com.au

Making the restructured thinking habitual

To get to a point where you are thinking in a healthier way, you need to go through a process of deliberately challenging your thinking. You need to overlearn to notice your automatic thoughts and then reframe them into a healthier and more accurate alternative thought. With practice, you will be able to challenge your thinking and adjust your automatic thoughts without giving it much attention. Eventually, you will not even have to do that because your core beliefs will be corrected to offer you a more accurate template of how the world works and how you fit into that world.

Targeting the assumptions

Let's not forget about those assumptions that underlie the errors you make in your thinking. You need to challenge those assumptions to completely correct your thinking. Remember, if the assumptions that underlie the error are shown to be wrong, there is every reason to abandon the logical error and replace it with a more logical point of view.

There are a few ways you can challenge the assumptions that underlie logical errors. We are going to focus on three approaches. Firstly, we are going to apply the strategy of looking at the advantages and disadvantages of holding an assumption. Consider the following example of someone who always has to be right.

Logical error and assumption
Always being right. People have to choose a side, and there is a right side and a wrong side.
Advantages
It is satisfying to be proven right.
Disadvantages
I will be facing a lot of conflict with people if I continue to assume I am always right.   *I will be disappointed throughout life if I am not more flexible in my thinking.*   *There are lots of situations in life where there is no right and wrong side and I am going to have a difficult life if I don't accept this.*

Challenging the assumption that underlies a tendency to want to always be right, you can see that there are many more disadvantages to doing this than there are advantages. The disadvantages indicate that the holder of the assumption is facing ongoing difficulties if they continue to hold this point of view.

Secondly, you can act against the assumptions. What would happen if the assumption was incorrect? Consider the following example.

Logical error and assumption
Always being right. People have to choose a side, and there is a right side and a wrong side.
Things that might happen if I acted like the assumption was not true
I might relax instead of fighting for my point of view all the time.
I might find that I have fewer conflicts with people.
I might feel less of a burden of responsibility to be in charge of everything.

By acting as if the assumption is false, you can usually identify the positive things that would occur as a consequence. All of these things are better than fighting to be right about everything. Remember, trying always to be right is stressful and exhausting.

Finally, you can argue against the assumption. You can take the perspective that the assumption is wrong and develop an argument for your case. Consider the following example.

Logical error and assumption
Always being right. People have to choose a side, and there is a right side and a wrong side.
Arguments against the assumption
It is not possible to always be right about everything.
People are entitled to their own opinions.
There are lots of things in life that are a matter of point of view, so they are not a matter of right or wrong.

Here, you are thinking of the *facts* that can be used to present a good argument that the assumption associated with the logical error is not accurate. This will allow you to challenge your error-ridden thinking and replace it with healthier thinking that will not encourage you to feel strong, negative emotions.

Below is a worksheet you can use to challenge the assumptions that underlie your errors in thinking.

Targeting assumptions worksheet
Logical error and assumption
Advantages
Disadvantages
Things that might happen if I acted like the assumption was not true
Arguments against the assumption

Worksheet is available at elemen.com.au

Here, we have asked you to consider challenging the sorts of thoughts you might have that are likely to make you feel worse than you would otherwise feel if you did not think that way. You have learned to access these logical errors by paying attention to your automatic thoughts that serve as the running commentary your mind provides. You have learned ways to challenge these errors and remove them and their influence from your thinking. The goal of doing these things has been to help you manage your distress and protect yourself from distress in the future.

Now we need to consider how you can move forward with your new, healthier thinking style. It is important now to start to consider what you want and how your life might change for the better.

Restoring your sense of self

One important step in determining what you want to change in your life and in what direction your life should go is to consider who you are and what you stand for. We have already discussed what it means to have a strong sense of self and why this is desirable. For some, that strong sense of self has always been evident. For others, they may struggle to develop this sense of self as being separate from what others expect of them. However, even if you do not currently have a good sense of self, it is possible to work on this.

Focusing on restoring your sense of self is particularly important in cases where your sense of self has shifted. What you thought you knew about yourself seems no longer to apply. It may be necessary to re-establish your values and identify what it is you know about yourself now that your priorities have shifted or your roles have changed.

How to build a strong sense of self

It is entirely possible to develop a stronger and clearer sense of self. In fact, to be fulfilled in life, it may be necessary to do so. Without it, you may struggle to feel settled, confident and content.

Let's consider some ways to promote a good sense of self.

Clarify your values

Your personal beliefs about you and life and the values you hold are fundamental aspects of who you are as a person. These things assist you in determining what position you take in relation to important issues and can influence what you might choose to do to express your values (e.g., work hard, devote yourself to family, protest, volunteer). Clarification of your values can help you set limits or establish boundaries. For example, if honesty is something of value to you, you may choose not to spend time with people who have a loose relationship with the truth. If you are unsure what your values are, then you may spend some time considering what you want to stand for. Remember, determine what you stand for, not what you think others believe you should stand for.

> *Anthony knew the time had come for him to work out what he stood for. He had been raised in a dysfunctional family, and his childhood was marred by the alcohol and drug use of his parents. In general, his extended family held antisocial attitudes that resulted in criminal actions by family members that were applauded by other people within the family. Anthony had been on the periphery of this life throughout his childhood and adult life up until this point. He now wanted something different for himself and his own family. He decided a law-abiding life was what he needed, separate from the influences of other family members. He did not want his children to think it was all right to act like their grandparents, aunts, uncles and cousins. Although he was ridiculed by family members for this decision, Anthony felt much better about himself now that he had completely rejected the values his family had tried to instil in him.*

Learn to care for and nurture yourself

To take care of yourself you have to pay attention to your needs. In doing so, you are making an effort to understand yourself and what you need in life. We often just ignore what we need as we go about our daily lives. We give little consideration to what we need to be all right. By focusing our attention on what we need, we are taking action to feel more connected with ourselves, knowing what we need to do to make ourselves feel better.

> *For most of her adult life so far, Tanya has focused on the needs of others. The problem was that she had done this to her own detriment. She never put herself and her needs first. Now, she felt exhausted by the demands of others who had come to expect she would do what they needed and wanted. So, Tanya made a decision to have a more balanced approach to her life. She started walking with a friend, she returned to hobbies she had enjoyed but abandoned years ago, and she handed over some household tasks to her husband and teenaged children. Tanya wanted more time for herself, and she realised it was reasonable to take this time.*

Make choices for yourself

It is important to start to make decisions that benefit you. This does not stop you from also making choices that benefit other important people in your life, such as your partner or children. However, those choices should not diminish the importance of the choices you make for yourself.

If you are a person who does things for others to the exclusion of doing things for yourself, it might be difficult to shift your thinking to considering your own wellbeing. The best approach is to start doing this in smaller ways until you learn that you can both make choices that benefit you and also consider the needs of your loved ones.

> *George always went along with what others decided. He used to laugh and say he was a follower rather than a leader. However, by putting others in the driver's seat of his life, he ended up doing things he wouldn't have chosen for himself. His friends took him fishing and camping, and he went even though he hated both activities. He spent lots of time working in the garden. This was an activity that his wife loved, but he hated. His children chose the TV shows he watched. He chose books to read that his workmates recommended. George decided enough was enough. Although engaging in these activities pleased others, he realised they did not make him happy. So, he made the decision that he was going to start to do the things that he wanted with the free time he had available to him. He started taking art classes, and he joined a local amateur drama club. Those who thought they knew him were surprised by his choices. They had assumed that George had been happy because he had never told them otherwise. He still helped his wife in the garden and spent time with his friends. He still supported his children's right to choose regarding TV-watching, within reason. However, he also started making choices for himself that catered to his own needs and he started to feel much more content as a result.*

Establish a good support network

In making choices for yourself that meet your needs, you are not required to ignore the advice of others. People who are supportive of us can help us understand what they see in us. That is, we can see the best in ourselves if we have people in our lives who see the best in us. This can help you develop a good sense of self.

A strong social network may be made up of people who share similar faith or a similar philosophy of life. This can help us build confidence in our views of ourselves and, thus, help us develop a strong sense of self.

> *Roslyn had a lot of people in her life. Most of the people were acquaintances, and quite a few of them had strong opinions. They tended to tell Roslyn what she should be doing. She knew these people wanted what was best for her, but they tended to give advice based on what was suitable from their own perspectives. Roslyn decided that these were not the people who could offer her the best support, even if their intentions were good. Slowly, over time, she began to foster relationships with people who took the time to know her properly and whom she could rely on to offer the best advice. She did not reject the other people in her life. She continued to enjoy their company without relying on them for support.*

Learn to be comfortable spending time alone

Spending time alone can help you better understand yourself. It allows you to reflect on what you want and need without the influence of others around you who might express opinions or make demands in ways that encourage you to come in line with what they want.

Some people enjoy time alone. For others, this can be quite a challenge. Being around people all the time allows you not to have to think about yourself, your needs, and your values. However, spending time alone does not mean that you must spend that time solely on self-reflection. It allows you to explore the things that interest you and understand that the decisions you make to engage in various activities are yours alone.

> *Sandra had a busy life. She was always surrounded by others. There were always teenagers in her home who were friends of her own teenaged children. Family members visited regularly with their children. She had a part-time job that involved her dealing with the public. Friends would drop in, and weekends were often spent barbecuing with groups of friends and family members. Sandra was always on the go and never had any time for herself. She didn't really have much experience being alone, and it struck her that she would find it difficult to be by herself because her life had been so full of people. She realised that her relying on others to fill her day was going to present a problem if a time came when various people were not available to her. So, Sandra made a decision to take some time for herself. People initially didn't understand her reasoning, but she insisted that she wanted some time to reflect on her own thoughts. Although it was challenging at first, Sandra learned that this time to herself gave her a sense of peace and quiet that had been missing in her life. It also gave her a better understanding of herself in a way that surprised her. She realised that because she had been surrounded by lots of chatter in her life, she had never really considered her own thoughts about various things and life in general.*

Allow yourself to heal from past hurts

One way of building your sense of self is to resolve past hurts or reconcile past wrongs. These types of issues in our past tend to undermine our self-confidence. Our view of ourselves tends to focus more on what happened to us rather than who we are as a person. By coming to terms with what has happened, we are able to spend more time thinking about what we want to represent us with regard to our values and our view of life than reflecting on things from the past to the extent that they consume our thoughts.

> *Leo had spent a lot of time feeling bitter about the end of his marriage. The thoughts about how he had been wronged were all-consuming. These thoughts coloured how he saw the world. In general, he saw the world as a nastier place than he had before the breakdown of his marriage. His bitterness influenced the choices he made. He avoided friendships and did not pursue a romantic relationship because he felt all people were untrustworthy. However, over time, Leo began to realise that this focus on his bitterness was limiting his life. He had lost sight of what mattered to him and what made him happy. He knew he had to let go of this bitterness. He began to accept that his past relationship was history. He realised there was no point in continuing to be hurt about something he could not change. By allowing it to continue to affect him, he realised that the only person being hurt was him. He needed to focus on the future, and he knew that he couldn't do that while he was hanging on to past hurtful events. He began to understand that he did not want his life defined by this one bad experience.*

Plan to achieve your goals and live life the way you want

We have known for some time that the discrepancies between who you are and how you are living your life, who you want to be, and how you want to live your life can result in feelings of dissatisfaction and discontent.

In exploring your sense of self, you are taking the first step away from that internal conflict. However, you need to consider how that knowledge of who you are is going to translate into changes in your life so that you are living the type of life that is consistent with that sense of who you are as a person. Think about ways your newly identified sense of self can determine your life direction. You are asking yourself not only who you are but also what you want to do.

> *Lance wanted things to change. He had been living a life that no longer made him happy. He knew that if he didn't make a change, he would regret it later on. But what he wanted to do risked some of the things that were important to him. In particular, he worried about the financial security of his family. This worried him enough to make him question the wisdom of making any changes in his life. Lance wanted to start a consulting business, offering advice to businesses about how to restructure their companies with the goal of improving productivity and achieving good outcomes. He knew that giving up his paid employment to start his own consultancy business was risky. So, he made a plan to transition to his new role. He decided to work extra hours outside of his paid employment to start to build a reputation. As his client base increased, he decided he would cut back his hours of paid employment and would continue to work part-time in his current job until he had built up his own business to the point where it was profitable and could sustain him and his family financially. He knew that this would involve hard work for a while, but he was excited about having a plan that would allow him to pursue his goals without too great a risk.*

Bear in mind that it is normal enough to experience changes in your sense of self. Remember that your view of yourself as a teenager is not the same as your view of yourself later in life. You should allow yourself to develop in a way that allows your sense of self to naturally shift to one that is relevant to the stage of life you are in.

Improving your quality of life

In addressing your sense of self and trying to formulate an idea of where you want your life to head, it can be difficult to understand your values. It is hard to decide what aspects of your life need changing.

Moving forward with the intention of doing things differently, it is important that you choose activities that are meaningful to you and that will improve the satisfaction you feel with your life. It is easy to fill your life with things to do, even leisure activities. However, not all of these potential activities will give you a sense of satisfaction. This is because not all activities are important to you. If you are going to make improvements in your life, you should choose activities that are of high value to you.

How do you know what activities would contribute the most to improving the quality of your life? We often do not think about what we value as we go through our busy day and the question of what a person values can often be confounding to them. Borrowing from a particular therapy called Acceptance and Commitment Therapy, we have included here an exercise in values clarification that will help you decide which activities would be of the greatest value to you.

The goal of this exercise is to identify ways you can put into your life the things that you value the most. The purpose of doing this is to improve your quality of life by having more things in your life that matter to you the most.

When we refer to the things you value, we are not referring to a specific activity. For example, you may have a value related to spending more time with your family. A specific activity that might flow from this value is to have a meal with your family once a week.

Below is a diagram that contains labels for various life domains. A life domain is an area of your life that reflects one portion of who you are and what you do. This is an example of what we are talking about when we refer to your life domain map.

Values clarification exercise for choosing preferred activities

Step 1 involves you listing as many life domains as you can think of that are relevant to you. We have included some life domains that people often list, but feel free to change them and add new ones that are relevant to you. What you are doing here is building your life domain map. Take your time to think up as many life domains as you understand to be part of your life. Other examples might be travel, exercise, etc.

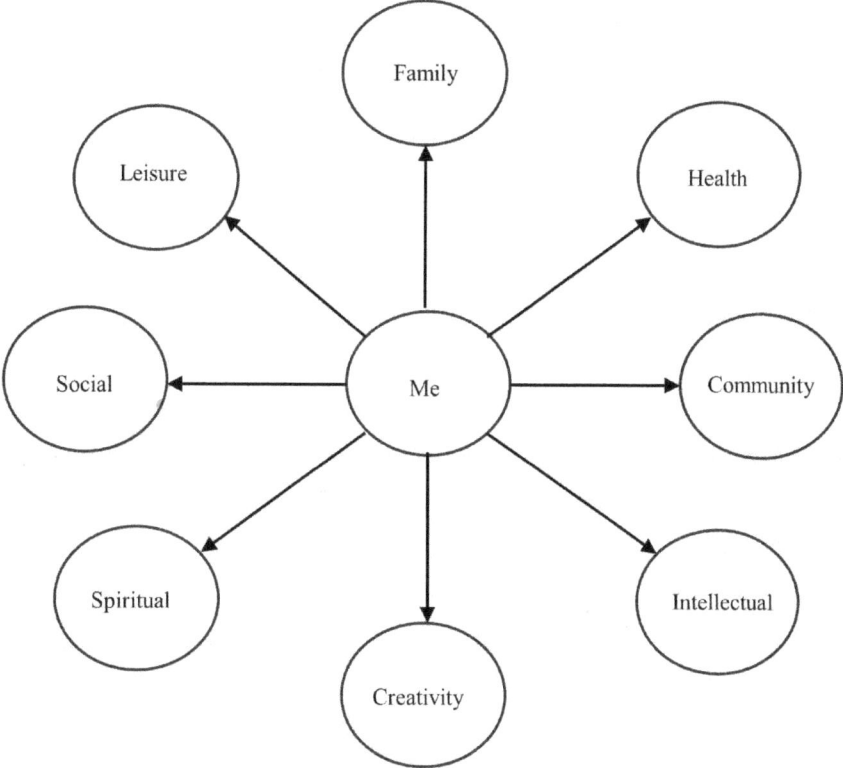

Figure 9: An example of a life domain map.

Step 2 involves you identifying what you already have in your life for the various life domains. Remember, list the values you have (e.g., ample time with your family) rather than specific activities (e.g., Sunday lunch with your family). You will begin to notice that some domains in your life have received lots of attention, but other domains have received little or no attention. Here is an example of the types of values that might appear in the family domain.

    Family domain:

        Time with family

        Special time with individual family members

        Spending time with the young members of my family

        Important family gatherings

Remember, you are listing here what you already have of value in your life with regard to this domain. This is not a list of the things you would like to have available to you.

Step 3 involves you now considering the things you would like to have in your life in each of the domains. Again, focus on the values (e.g., more quality time with my parents) rather than activities (e.g., visiting my parents on Sunday afternoons).

At this point, you will begin to notice several things.

> You will see that there are domains of your life that receive lots of attention already and you want very little else in that domain. Things in these domains are already satisfactory, so there is limited purpose in focusing your attention on them.
>
> You will see that there are domains of your life where you have very little but you also do not really want very much more. These do not deserve your attention either.
>
> Importantly, you will see there are domains of your life where you have very little, and there are many things that you want in that domain that you do not already have available to you. Focusing your attention on these would give you the greatest benefit.

It is the third type of life domain that will become the focus of attention from here on. This is because this focus will have the greatest chance of having the most important impact on the quality of your life.

Step 4 involves focusing on those life domains where you do not have enough of what matters to you, and there is very much more that you want to include in your life. In this step, you should consider how those values that you want to put into your life might translate into specific activities. It is here that the 'what to do' component of the exercise occurs. For example, if you have a value associated with spending more time with your family, you might now consider ways that could happen by identifying specific activities you could engage in that would bring that value into your life (e.g., arranging family get-togethers, organising an online shared family photo site where family members can post photos for all family members to see).

Step 5 involves identifying any barriers that might prevent you from engaging in these activities that would bring the things that you value into your life and finding ways around these barriers. For example, you may not be able to catch up in person with family members if they live in places distant from you, but you could overcome this barrier by arranging video chat get-togethers.

Of course, there will be things you want that are of value to you that you just cannot have because of real limitations. For example, you may like to travel but cannot do so for a variety of reasons. However, if travel is of high value, then the quality of your life might be enhanced by spending time exploring places online or watching travel documentaries. Although not exactly what you would give the highest value, these activities are still related to the thing that matters to you.

Remember that your goal is to introduce into your life activities that are of high value to you that will improve the quality of your life. If you are going to devote the time to engaging in these types of activities, it will matter that you focus on the activities that are associated with your highest values.

Planning a future

The time has come to consider the future you want to have available to you. We are not going to tell you what that future will look like or what you should choose. We are going to give you some simple advice about what you should do to begin your planning.

Stages of change

It is a good idea to spend some time thinking about what you want to change and, importantly when you want to change it. Not all changes have to occur at once. Instead, it makes sense to plan for your future in terms of your immediate plans, your middle-term plans, and your long-term plans.

When deciding on when your goals should be met, you can set a time frame. For example, you might want your immediate plans to be enacted in the next few months. Your mid-term plans could have a timeframe of up to a year or two years. Your longer-term plans might include what you want to achieve in the next five years.

The timeframes you set will be determined by you, as your individual goals will influence how long it will take you to achieve them. For example, your financial security, the independence of your children, or the need to retrain for a new career may impact the timing of your goals.

Adopt a problem-solving approach

It is important that you do not approach this planning for your future is a haphazard way. This process should not be based on ill-considered, impulsive guesswork. Although you cannot know with certainty how things will turn out when you make changes, it increases the chances of a good outcome if you approach the planning process in a structured way.

A good way of handling this challenge is to adopt a problem-solving approach to decision-making. A problem-solving approach uses defined actions with the aim of considering the potential outcomes of choices you make.

Let's consider the steps you can take to make decisions.

Define the problem you are facing

A problem is defined as any situation where you are faced with uncertainty about the direction you should take. It is important here to clearly define the problem you are considering. If you miss this step, your job will be much more difficult. It is hard to know what choice to make when you are not even sure what it is you should be addressing.

The way to go about this is to define the problem in concrete terms. By this, we mean defining the problem in language that clearly defines the problem you are facing rather than using terms that are general or could be applied to any situation.

Consider the following statements in terms of how useful they would be in a problem-solving context.

> Problem statement #1: *I just want things to be better.*
>
> Problem statement #2: *I want to make changes to my work life.*
>
> Problem statement #3: *I want to find a job where I can use my creative talents.*

Statement one is the most general statement. By saying you just want things to be better, you are presenting yourself with some difficulties that could be avoided if you made a more concrete statement. For example, by saying you want things to be better, you are not specifying what it is you want to improve, you are not indicating what you mean by 'better', and you have no way of knowing when this 'better' state has been achieved. The last point is a particularly important one. How can you define success in any change process if you cannot identify what it is you are hoping to achieve?

Statement two narrows things down. It goes part of the way to stating what it is you want to focus on. Rather than just wanting things to be better, you now at least know that the focus should be on your work life. However, it has not yet gone far enough. When trying to determine a way forward, it is not clear what aspect of work life needs to be changed. The result might be that you would go down unhelpful pathways in trying to change your life.

By clarifying that it is about your work life that you want to change, Statement three allows you to start to consider how to achieve this specific goal. Not only is the pathway to achieving this goal easier, by clearly clarifying your goal, you would be able to know if and when that goal is achieved.

It is worth mentioning here that it is better to apply this problem-solving approach to a variety of aspects of the changes you make in life separately rather than approaching this process in a more global way that attempts to incorporate all aspects of your life in a single attempt to problem-solve. So, when you are defining the problem, choose specific aspects of the changes you want to consider in your life.

Generate a list of possible solutions

After identifying the problem on which you want to focus, the next step is to generate a list of the ways you could address the problem. The idea here is to generate as comprehensive a list as possible. This list might comprise possible solutions that you have thought up yourself, a list of solutions that you have generated with the help of friends or a combination of both.

This list needs to include all the possible ways forward you can imagine. Even though you will later rule out some options, you do not want to limit yourself here. Sometimes, things that you want that you do not think are possible can seem more likely to be successful after you consider how you might make them work.

Let's generate a list about changing your job to make use of your creative skills.

> I could look for a job that makes creative products.
>
> I could quit my job and start up my own business, making creative products for sale.
>
> I could undertake some training in running a business before changing jobs.
>
> I could start small and sell some of the creative things I have produced while still working in my current job, with the goal of transitioning into this new work life.

Although there are probably many more options available that could be considered, this list is adequate for the purposes of learning how to use a problem-solving approach to finding a pathway forward.

Evaluate options for likelihood of success

Once your list of possible solutions has been generated, the next step is to evaluate them for the likelihood of their success in terms of your long-term goal. Remember, for the sake of this learning exercise, the goal is to find a job that makes use of your creative skills. Let's evaluate the items on the list we generated.

I could look for a job that makes creative products.
This seems like a good idea but such a job might be hard to find. I do not only want to work for a creative business, I want to be doing creative things. Not only might such a job be hard to find, a job that focuses on my particular creative skills might be even more difficult to secure. I would not rule out this option but it seems that this might rely on luck rather than me controlling the changes in my life.
I could quit my job and start up my own business, making creative products for sale.
This seems like a risky thing to do. I have heard that most new small businesses fail. I would like my own business but I would not want to threaten my financial wellbeing by doing something risky.
I could undertake some training in running a business before changing jobs.
This seems like a good idea. It would undoubtedly help me in the longer term if I started up a business of my own. However, the idea of focusing on learning about how businesses run seems to delay my goal of being employed doing something creative. I really want to do something now.

> I could start small and sell some of the creative things I have produced while still working in my current job, with the goal of transitioning into this new work life.
>
> *This seems like a cautious approach, but it may be the wisest. I could build up a customer base. I could also find out what sells and what does not so that my creative efforts are directed towards something that would generate retail interest. It would allow me to learn what I need to know but also give me the satisfaction of doing the things I really want to do.*

Choose a preferred option

The next step is to choose the pathway you want to take. In a normal problem-solving process, where you are dealing with a dilemma you are facing, you typically choose the best option with the greatest likelihood of success and then move forward and apply the solution you have chosen.

However, when you are using this problem-solving process to help you plan your future, you may choose more than one option. It can work well if you combine your option selection with the stages of change approach. That is, you can select an option for your immediate goals, your middle-term goals and your longer-term goals.

Let's consider the example we have been using.

> Immediate goals
>
> *I will choose to start small and sell some of the creative things I have produced while still working in my current job, with the goal of transitioning into this new work life. By doing this, I am not risking my financial security, but I am meeting my need to be doing something straight away. This is likely to encourage me on my pathway to a new career.*
>
> Middle-term goals
>
> *I will undertake some training that I might need to successfully run a new business. In this way, I could learn about the pitfalls I need to avoid as well as the specific skills that I do not yet have that will increase the chances that my business will be successful.*
>
> Longer-term goals
>
> *My longer-term goal will be to start up my own small business. I can build on my established customer base that I developed by selling some of my creative products along the way. When the time is right, I can quit my job but have a growing business to step into.*

Evaluate effectiveness

The final step in this problem-solving process is to evaluate the effectiveness of the option or options you have selected and implemented. To do this, it is worthwhile operationalising your outcomes. This means you clearly identify, in concrete terms, what you would consider to be an indicator of success. So, rather than saying to yourself, "I think this is working", and then hoping that it is, you can identify success when, for example, your products are selling, your profit margin is comfortable, and the demand exists. You can probably think of other objective indicators of success.

If you evaluate the effectiveness of the pathways you have chosen and you are not happy with the outcome, all is not lost. You could choose to brainstorm other options that could be available to you, evaluate their likely success and then evaluate their effectiveness when you implement them.

Building a flexible plan

It is important that any plan you have for your future is flexible. This is because any plan is speculative in nature rather than factual. Even though you may have thought through the possible consequences of your plan and arrived at a likely outcome, you still have to wait to see how things will work out.

It may be necessary to adjust your plan to accommodate new information that you had not considered when you made your plan. A rigid plan will not allow you to do this. A rigid plan is either successful or fails. It cannot be adjusted along the way. A flexible plan will provide you with the opportunity to take into account new information, reject aspects of the plan that are not working, and build on aspects of the plan that are successful.

Below is a worksheet you can use to make some future plans.

Future plan worksheet
What is the problem I am facing?
Here is a list of possible ways I could address this problem.
What is the likelihood that I will be satisfied with the outcome of each approach?
I choose this option for solving the problem.
Now that I have implemented my problem-solving option, how effective was it?
Now that I have implemented my problem-solving option, is there anything I could do that would improve the outcome?

Worksheet available at elemen.com.au

Using this worksheet can help you to clarify a pathway forward and help you adapt your plan to achieve the best possible outcome.

Some final thoughts

Here, we would like to take the opportunity to highlight some points that you should remember as you go through this period of your life.

> It is normal to go through periods of change in your life. This happens throughout your life and is a reflection of normal developmental processes. What you want at one point in your life may not be what you want at another point.
>
> It is unsettling to face change. However, this unsettled feeling is not a sign of dysfunction or psychological instability. This is true even if the unsettled feeling is uncomfortable or if you are feeling negative emotions that are not normally a part of your typical psychological state. The unsettled feeling just means you are being challenged to change direction in your life.
>
> This period of transition can seem confusing. This is because the way forward may not always be clear. As with any change, you need to give consideration to what you want and how you might go about achieving it. Once a plan is developed, that feeling of confusion typically passes.
>
> Change can be healthy and good as long as it is handled well. Acting impulsively and without consideration for how things are likely to turn out will not be the wisest thing to do. Thoughtful consideration is preferable to rushing headlong into an uncertain future.
>
> You should enjoy a life of good quality. How that is defined is likely to differ from person to person. However, even people faced with real challenges in their lives can still have a life of good quality. This is achieved by maximising the positive experiences and minimising negative aspects.

We wish you well for the future.

Additional readings

Eifer, G.H., Forsyth, J.P., & Hayes, S.C. (2005). *Acceptance and commitment therapy for anxiety disorders.* New York: New Harbinger Publications.

Kennerley, H., Kirk, J., & Westbrook, D. (2016). *An introduction to cognitive behaviour therapy: Skills and applications (3rd edn.).* London: Sage Publications.

Sears, R.W. (2021). *The sense of self: Perspectives from science and Zen Buddhism.* Springer Nature.

www.ingramcontent.com/pod-product-compliance
Lightning Source LLC
Chambersburg PA
CBHW080856090426
42735CB00014B/3162